Switched-On
SCHOOLHOUSE®

Program Guide
and Teacher Manual

ALPHA OMEGA
PUBLICATIONS

www.aop.com

Printed in the United States of America

ISBN 0-7403-0358-9

TABLE OF CONTENTS

CHAPTER 7: TECHNICAL INFORMATION 117

CHAPTER 8: LIFEPAC COMPARISON 133

CHAPTER 9: OUR PHILOSOPHY OF EDUCATION 139

CHAPTER 10: SOFTWARE LICENSE AGREEMENT 141

INDEX 144

Chapter I

INSTALLATION AND SET UP

The following gives step-by-step instructions to get you started in Switched-On Schoolhouse.

Switched-On Schoolhouse is a powerful educational tool designed to reduce the teacher's administrative load and improve student academics.

Using the Schoolhouse, you will be able to do the same things you did with a paper curriculum—and more! From designing your own projects to skipping lessons or re-arranging units, you can customize the Schoolhouse to fit your needs.

If you are new to the Schoolhouse, take some time to familiarize yourself with how it works. You can set up a practice student and play around with all the options before setting up your real students. Then you can delete  your practice student once you are comfortable with the program.

Switched-On Schoolhouse comes with default settings already in place. However, you may want to adjust some of the settings to customize the program for your particular students and for your teaching style.

If you have used the Schoolhouse in previous years, get acquainted with the new and improved features.

New for the 2001 School Year:

- Alternate tests (Bible, History, Language Arts, Science, Health Quest)
- Quiz/test solution keys in Math 9–12
- Vocabulocity II (Alpha 14)
- New Dynamic Learning Activities (DLAs): Math, Science, History
- Timeline
- Open calendar
- Welcome videos with study tips
- More multimedia
- New themes

INSTALLATION

You will need to (1) install the program and (2) install each subject. (Instructions follow.)

Note: Close all other programs, including screen savers, before installing and running Switched-On Schoolhouse. This will keep the programs from competing with each other.

Step 1 – Install program:

Insert CD-ROM (Disk "A" of any multi-CD subject) in CD drive. | Double-click on My Computer | Double-click on D:\ drive (if "D" is your CD drive). | Double-click on Install.exe and follow the on-screen instructions.

Installation Options:

```
Installation Options
 ○ Install This Subject Only: Does not copy code or multimedia.
 ○ Minimal: needs 10MB.  Does not install Spelling Bee, Vocabulocity, Introduction Videos, Themes.
              Warning: with Minimal install, Vocabulocity and Spelling Bee will be disabled!
 ○ Small: needs 35MB.  Does not install Introduction Videos, Themes.
 ○ Full: needs 93MB.  All features enabled.
 ◉ Install Student on Network: Enter mapped network drive below.

   Location on Hard Drive / Network Drive
   F:\                              [  Uninstall  ]        [  Install  ]   [  Cancel  ]
```

Switched-On Schoolhouse installation provides five
installation options. The choices "Minimal," "Small," and
"Full" all install Switched-On Schoolhouse (code) to
your computer. Choose one of these options if you are
installing for the first time or if you are installing a newer
version. In general, "Full" installation is recommended
because it contains all the features, including multimedia
enhancements and games. The option "Install This
Subject Only" should be used when you already have
the latest version of Switched-On Schoolhouse installed
on your computer and you are merely adding a new
subject. The option "Install Student on Network" is for
use with a Local Area Network (see *Advanced Setup*).
Select an installation based on the amount of hard drive
space you have on your computer.

Location on Hard Drive. Unless you specify
otherwise, Switched-On Schoolhouse will be installed to
"C:\SOS" (a folder labeled "SOS" on your C:\ drive). All
information pertaining to Switched-On Schoolhouse
and your students' work will go into the SOS folder.
Note: This path is a DOS path, not a Windows path.

Step 2 – Install individual subjects:

To install another subject:

Insert CD-ROM (Disk "A" of any multi-CD subject) in
CD drive. | Double-click on My Computer | Double-
click on D:\ drive (if "d" is your CD drive) | Double-

click on Install.exe and follow the on-screen instructions. Choose "Install This Subject Only." Repeat these steps for all subjects.

Once you have installed the program and all the subjects, you are ready to set up the school and your students.

Before Setting Up

Before setting up your school and your students, you need to learn about Student Mode and Teacher Mode.

Student Mode / Teacher Mode

Students and teachers share the same menus but access different controls. In Teacher Mode, teachers can access all controls, curriculum, and answer keys. It is in Teacher Mode where teachers need to complete the set up for their students.

To get to Teacher Mode from the opening screen (Student Menu), scroll down until you see an
icon that says, "Go To Teacher Mode." Click on the Go To Teacher Mode icon. To get back to Student Mode, click on the Go To Student Mode icon. This concept is key to understanding the Switched-On Schoolhouse system; you are always in either Teacher Mode or Student Mode, and you need to return to the starting menu to switch between them. (See diagram on p.17.)

Note: You can tell when you are in Teacher Mode because the background says "Teacher Mode."

SETTING UP

To get started you will need to complete:

Part 1– Set up the school: (1) enter a Teacher Password, and (2) set the calendar for the school.

Part 2 – Set up the students: (1) add student names to the program, (2) assign students their work, (3) assign student passwords, and (4) create lesson plans.

Part 1: SCHOOL SETUP

To set up the teacher password and school calendar, you need to be in School Setup.

To get to School Setup:

• Click on Go to Teacher Mode.
• Click on School Setup.

1. Teacher Password:

The teacher password is needed to block students from the answer key and teacher controls.

In School Setup:

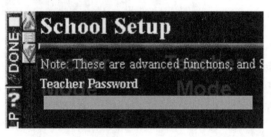

Make up a password and type it in the box labeled "Teacher Password" at the top of the screen. (If you forget your password, you can access Teacher Mode by holding down the shift key and clicking on the Go To Teacher icon. This action will erase the teacher's password and allow you to type a new teacher password.

2. Set Calendar for School:

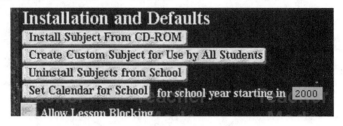

The school calendar is used to generate lesson plans.

In School Setup:

• Click on Set Calendar for School. (Change the starting calendar year if you need to.)

• For each calendar month, select all days appropriate to your school's schedule. Click a box to select. Click again to deselect. (Time-saving tip: Choose Load Default 180-Day Calendar at the top of the screen; then make changes to the calendar days.)

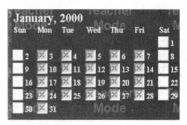

• Click DONE on the toolbar to save. The School Setup menu will display.

Note: To save changes in School Setup select DONE on the toolbar or press the ESC key. If you do not want to save changes, click EXIT on the toolbar. Selecting DONE will save your changes and take you back to the Teacher Menu. From the Teacher Menu you can add your students.

Part 2: STUDENT SETUP

You will set up students one at a time. Follow these steps in order for each of your students.

1. Add Student:

• Click on Go to Teacher Mode.

• Click on Add Student.

• Type in the student's name and click OK. Student Setup for that student will display.

• If you are following these instructions in order, note that Steps 2–4 below will take place in Student Setup, so stay on this screen. You will assign subjects and customize the program for each student in their respective Student Setup menus.

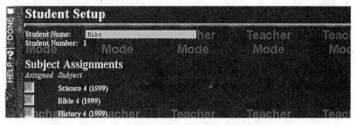

Note: You can have up to five students in the Home version of Switched-On Schoolhouse.

2. Assign Subject(s):

In Student Setup:

Note: When you add additional subjects you will need to return to Student Setup for the appropriate student in order to assign the new subjects.

The listing of available subjects is displayed below the student's name at the top of the screen. The box beside the subject assigns it. When selected, the box is indented.

• Click on the box next to the subject to assign it.

Note: When you add additional subjects you will need to return to Student Setup for the appropriate student in order to assign the new subjects.

3. Assign Student Password:

In Student Setup:

• Type a password in the box labeled "Student Password." (This is optional, but recommended for multiple student situations.)

4. Create Lesson Plans:

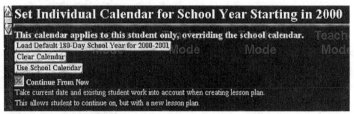

Switched-On Schoolhouse generates lesson plans based on the calendar you have made and the subjects you have assigned.

In Student Setup:

• Click on Create Lesson Plan, double-checking to make sure the year listed is correct.

• Choose either your school calendar (if you have set one up), the default calendar that came with the program, or simply click on the individual days to select them. Time saving tip: use the school calendar or default calendar; then modify the days needed for this particular student.

• If you are adding to a current student's lesson plan, check the box labeled Continue From Now. See *Lesson Plans* for more details.

• Click DONE to save the changes and go back to the Student Setup menu.

• Click DONE again to go back to the Teacher Menu where you can add another student or go to Student Mode.

Starting School

Once the basic student setup is complete, students can access their lessons and begin work. Students should read

the section Student Orientation before they get started.
Note: Teachers should familiarize themselves with both
Student and Teacher Mode before students start
working. Create a practice student that you can "play
with." Learn what it is like to be a student. Practice
grading. See *Teacher Orientation* for further suggestions.

CONTROLS

The side toolbar will help you move around in
Switched-On Schoolhouse. The controls and their
alternate keyboard commands are:

DONE (or **Esc** key) takes you back to the
previous (higher) menu.

SCROLL BAR moves the screen up and
down when you click and drag in either
direction.

HELP (or **F1**) opens the Help file.

NEXT (or **F2** or **right-click**) goes to the
next presentation or problem.

UTIL (or **F3**) displays a list of utilities.
You can then choose between custom functions,
problem helps, printing, and autohighlight.

QUIT (or **F4**) exits Switched-On Schoolhouse.

KEY (**Shift Key** or **F5**) displays the answer
key. F5 "locks" the answer key open.

Other keyboard controls that can be used in
Switched-On Schoolhouse include:

PAUSE key (or **CTRL M**) displays the
subject-specific message box while a student is
in a lesson.

CTRL Click on a student's name on the Teacher Menu takes the teacher directly to Student Setup.

CTRL P while in Teacher Mode will print the screen or the lesson.

SHIFT Click on a unit button in the Grading Menu skips over the unit.

CTRL Click on a unit button in the Grading Menu returns the unit settings to the default settings.

SHIFT Click on a video graphic to play the video full-screen.

RIGHT-Click on a video graphic to play the video in a loop (i.e., plays repeatedly).

SHIFT Right-Click on a video to play the video repeatedly full screen.

Click on a Slide Show to go to the next slide. Full-screen Slide Shows let you scroll over large graphics by moving the mouse pointer to the edge of the screen.

The **mouse** pointer touching the edges of the screen moves the screen up, down, right, and left.

The **Cursor** or **Arrow** keys scroll the screen up, down, right, and left, except when you are in a "text entry" box.

Page Up/Page Down keys move the screen up and down a page.

Home/End keys move the screen to the beginning and end of the page, respectively.

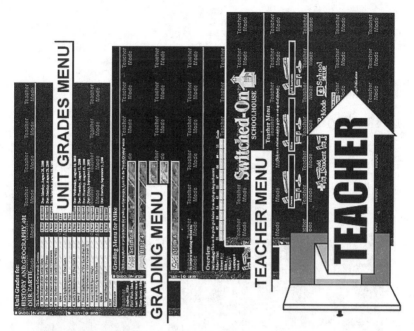

Student Mode / Teacher Mode. Students and teachers share the same menus but access different controls. In Teacher Mode, teachers can access all controls, curriculum, and answer keys. It is in Teacher Mode where teachers need to complete the setup for their students.

MENU OVERVIEWS

The menus in Teacher and Student modes are similar, but the teacher's menus contain more options and controls.

Teacher Mode

Teachers have access to three menus within the Teacher Mode: **Teacher Menu, Grading Menu,** and **Unit Grades Menu.**

I. Teacher Menu

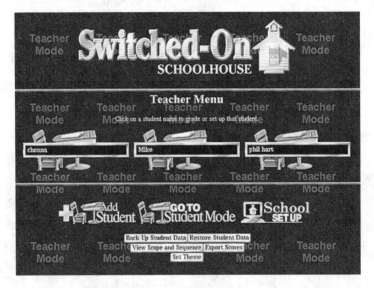

Click on **Go To Teacher Mode** to open the Teacher Menu. The Teacher Menu displays the class list with student names labeled on icons. From this menu teachers can add or delete students, enter School Setup, or access an individual student's work. We recommend that teachers set up a password to restrict access to the Teacher Menus. This can be done in School Setup.

From the Teacher Menu you can:

- See the complete class list.
- Add a student.
- Go To Student Mode.
- Go to School Setup.
- Back Up/Restore.
- View Scope and Sequence.
- Export Scores.
- Set theme for Teacher Mode.

2. Grading Menu

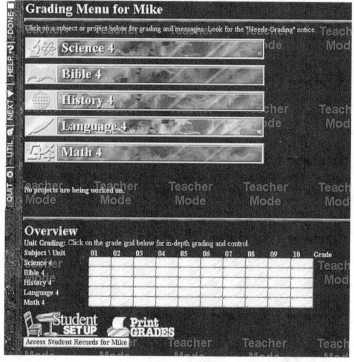

Click on a student's name in Teacher Mode to open the Grading Menu. This menu shows what the individual student is working on, what his current grades are, and what needs to be graded by the teacher.

From the Grading Menu you can:

- See assigned subjects.
- See "Past Due" and "Needs Grading" notices on the appropriate subjects; click on a subject icon to grade.
- Open Student Setup: name, password, assign subjects, customize.
- Print grades.
- Access Student Records.

3. Unit Grades Menu

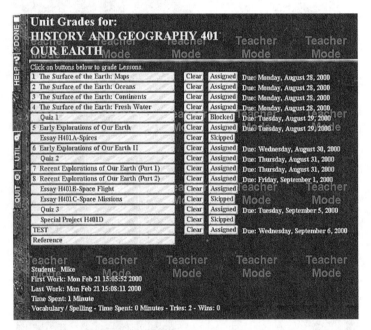

The Unit Grades Menu allows the teacher to take a closer look at the student's work.

Similar to opening a textbook to the Table of Contents, clicking on a unit button in the Grading Menu opens up a content list. The lesson titles are displayed as well as options to clear grades and assign or skip a lesson. By clicking on a particular lesson button, teachers can preview the content or review student work.

From the Unit Grades Menu you can:

- See the contents of the unit; view the presentations and problems.
- Customize a project.
- Print the lessons.
- Adjust grades, clear student work, skip problems, assign/skip/block lessons.
- View the due dates of individual lessons.
- View the total score, the unit grade, time spent in lessons, time and score of the games Vocabulocity and Spelling Bee, starting and ending times for student work in a unit

Student Mode

Students have limited access to the same three main menus as teachers do. In Student Mode the three menus are: **Student Menu**, **Schoolwork Menu**, and **Review Menu**.

I. Student Menu

The Student Menu displays the class list with the student names labeled on icons. Students click on their names to access their daily work.

In the Student Menu:

- If student passwords have been entered, students can gain access only to their own work.
- "Go To Teacher Mode" option is available (this option can be password-protected).
- Students can back up their schoolwork.

2. Schoolwork Menu

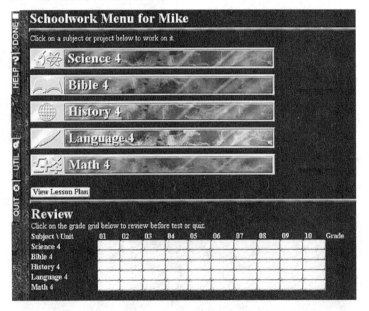

The Schoolwork Menu displays the student work assignments. To begin working, a student clicks on a subject or project bar.

In the Schoolwork Menu:

- Click on a subject or project bar to see messages, due dates, and study options.
- View current grades in unit grid below subject bars.

- Click on a button in the unit grid to review a completed unit.

- Set theme for student's desktop.

- View Lesson Plan.

3. Review Menu

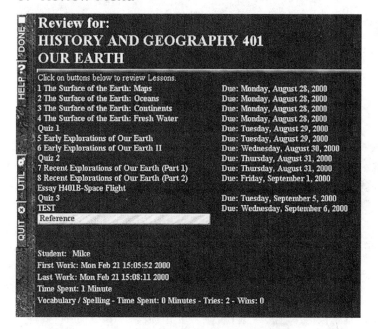

Review for:
HISTORY AND GEOGRAPHY 401
OUR EARTH

Click on buttons below to review Lessons.

1 The Surface of the Earth: Maps	Due: Monday, August 28, 2000
2 The Surface of the Earth: Oceans	Due: Monday, August 28, 2000
3 The Surface of the Earth: Continents	Due: Monday, August 28, 2000
4 The Surface of the Earth: Fresh Water	Due: Monday, August 28, 2000
Quiz 1	Due: Tuesday, August 29, 2000
5 Early Explorations of Our Earth	Due: Tuesday, August 29, 2000
6 Early Explorations of Our Earth II	Due: Wednesday, August 30, 2000
Quiz 2	Due: Thursday, August 31, 2000
7 Recent Explorations of Our Earth (Part 1)	Due: Thursday, August 31, 2000
8 Recent Explorations of Our Earth (Part 2)	Due: Friday, September 1, 2000
Essay H401B-Space Flight	
Quiz 3	Due: Tuesday, September 5, 2000
TEST	Due: Wednesday, September 6, 2000
Reference	

Student: Mike
First Work: Mon Feb 21 15:05:52 2000
Last Work: Mon Feb 21 15:08:11 2000
Time Spent: 1 Minute
Vocabulary / Spelling - Time Spent: 0 Minutes - Tries: 2 - Wins: 0

To review completed lessons, students can access their work through the Review Menu. Similar to opening a textbook to the Table of Contents, clicking on a unit button in the Schoolwork Menu opens up a content list. The lesson titles are displayed along with the grades earned. By choosing a particular lesson, students may see their completed work and review for the quizzes and tests. Students cannot, however, modify their work.

In the Review Menu:

- See the unit's table of contents, listing the lesson titles, reports, quizzes, and tests.

- View the presentations and problems that have already been completed.

- See grades and due dates.

BACK-UPS

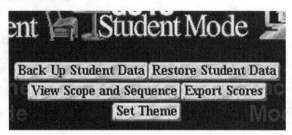

It is **very important** that the teacher (or student) maintains daily back-ups of student work. If something should happen to the computer's hard drive, all student work could be lost.

Switched-On Schoolhouse's built-in Back Up and Restore utility allows you to conveniently copy your students' work and grades onto a separate disk. "Back Up Student Data" copies student answers into a single large file. This file can be loaded on a floppy disk (or disks), a ZIP drive, a network, or on another hard drive.

BACK-UPS SHOULD BE MADE REGULARLY TO PROTECT AGAINST LOSS OF STUDENT WORK.

Detailed Back-up Instructions (Normal Operation)

1. Click on the Back Up Student Data button near the bottom of the Student Menu (opening screen) or on the Teacher Menu.

The following control will pop up:

Student Number:	All	Back Up
Subject:	All	☐ Prompt for each file
Unit Number:	All	Cancel

(See *Advanced Features* below for information on changing your options.)

2. Insert a blank, formatted floppy disk. You may need two or three if you have several students. **Note:** Switched-On Schoolhouse does not format or erase the floppy disk for you.

3. Click on the Back Up button. Another dialog box opens.

4. Click on OK to backup to the A: (floppy) drive, or select another location. The file name will be SOS.bak unless you change the name. The computer asks for another disk if it runs out of room.

5. Once the backup is complete, the program will confirm that the backup was successful. If all your backups fit onto one floppy disk you will not see the validation process unless a corrupt file is found. If your backup required multiple floppy disks, you will be prompted to reinsert them (order does not matter) for file validation. You can cancel the validation process at any time. If you do have a corrupt file on your floppy disk, run the backup again on a new floppy disk and throw the corrupt disk away. Do not use the corrupted disk. When the validation is complete you are told how many files were backed up. Keep back-up disks in a safe place.

Restore

If you ever need to restore a copy of your students' work (after a hard drive crash, for example), insert one of your back-up disks (the order is NOT important), click on the Restore Data button, then the Restore button, and select (click on) the file on your floppy disk when it asks for a file (sos.bak unless you changed the name). Click on OK. Repeat this process with any other back-up disks.

Advanced Features for Back Up/Restore

The advanced filter controls allow you to back up and restore specific parts of the student data.

• You can Back Up or Restore a single **student** by entering the desired student number at the line labeled "Student Number." (You can view the student number in Student Setup.)

• You can Back Up or Restore a specific **subject** by entering the subject name at the line labeled "Subject."

For example:

• You can type in the full name such as "history 8" or "Language 11" using either upper case or lower case letters.

• You can enter the actual directory name such as "bib0899" or "SCI1099."

• You can enter the first three letters of a subject to get all grades of that subject such as "bib," "his," "mat," "sci," or "lan."

• You may use upper or lower case letters. **Note:** For custom subjects you must use the "source" name (i.e.

the name of the subject CD-ROM, not the name you made up for the custom subject.)

- You can Back Up or Restore a specific **unit** by entering that unit number at the line labeled "Unit Number."

- If you check the "Prompt for each file" box, you will be asked to approve each file.

Note: You should at least do one full back-up (everything set to All) to record the school calendar, student names, and other data.

PRINTING

Student Grades:

1. Click on Go to Teacher Mode.
2. Click on a student's name.
3. Click on Print Grades (will print grades with semester grading).

Curriculum and Screen Shots:

1. Click on Go to Teacher Mode.
2. Hold down the CTRL key and press the P key OR click on UTIL on the toolbar and choose Print (screen shot) or Print Text (text only).

Vocabulary and Spelling Word Lists:

1. Click on Go to Teacher Mode.
2. Click on a student's name.
3. Click on the subject/unit in the Overview grade grid to open the Unit Grades Menu.
4. Click on the appropriate lesson.
5. Scroll down to the word list and click on Click Here to Copy/Print List.

Answer Key:

Follow steps I through 4 above, then:

5. Press F5 to lock the answer key open.

6. Hold down the CTRL key and press the P key.

ADVANCED SETUP

The advanced setup features include:

• Student-specific icons

• Customized Student Records

• Networked Student Data

Student-Specific Icons on the Desktop

You can set up a different icon for each of your students so that they can go directly to their Schoolwork menus. To do this:

1. Make another shortcut to Switched-On Schoolhouse. The shortcut is the light-switch icon on your desktop. You make a shortcut by right-clicking on it (clicking with the right mouse button) and choosing Create Shortcut from the menu that pops up. Another light-switch icon will appear on your desktop.

2. Right-click on the new shortcut and choose Properties from the menu that pops up.

3. In the line marked "Target" type a space after "C:\SOS\SOS.EXE" then type an "s" and the student number of the particular student for whom you are creating the shortcut.

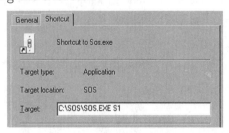

Examples:

> C:\SOS\SOS.EXE S1 will set up a direct link to the Schoolwork Menu of the student with the student number 1. C:\SOS\SOS.EXE S2 will set up a direct link to the Schoolwork Menu of the student with the student number 2. (You can find the student number by looking in the Student Setup of each student.)

4. Rename the icon to the name of your student. Right-click on the new icon and choose Rename from the menu that pops up. Type in the student's name.

Note: When the icons are set up for individual students, clicking "DONE" in the Schoolwork Menu returns the student to the Windows desktop instead of to the Student Menu.

Customized Student Records

Each student has an "Access Student Records" button on his or her Grading Menu. Click here to open a word processor document in which you can record additional information about your student. By default the link is made to the teacher's word processor program. Switched-On Schoolhouse does not add information to this file so you can do with it what you wish. Students do not have access to the Accent Student Records button; it is included for administrative use only.

You can change the "Access Student Records" button to connect to another program, such as a spreadsheet. To do so you need to complete steps 1 and 2 below.

Step 1 – Create a file in the program of your choice and name it as follows:

1. Create the document you want (word processor, spreadsheet, or other).
2. Save the document you created as template.xyz (where xyz is the file extension of your program) into the SOS folder on your hard drive.

   For example: template.doc (Microsoft Word document) or template.xls (Microsoft Excel document).

Note that there is already a file in the SOS folder called template.rtf. Template.rtf is the default word processing file used to create your student records.

Step 2 – Change the link.

1. Open the file called recordsx.lst in the SOS folder on your hard drive. You should see:

   **program=c:\progra~1\access~1\wordpad.exe
   extension=rtf
   directory=c:\sos\work\records**
   .

2. You will need to change the program and extension lines to that of the program you are linking. To find the proper path, use the "locate" button for the utility programs in School Setup. The program path that Switched-On Schoolhouse "Locate" enters into the location line is the program path you need for the records.lst file. Type this exact path into the line "program=" and change the line "extension=" to the proper extension.

Note: Do not delete the period at the end of the list. For example:

   **program=c:\progra~1\micros~3\office\excel.exe
   extension=xls
   directory=c:\sos\work\records**
   .

3. Save the altered recordsx.lst file as records.lst.

Note: If you delete the line "program=" the system uses the teacher's word processor. If the line "extension=" is deleted, the system defaults to the **.rtf** extension. If the line "directory=" is deleted, the default directory c:\sos\work\records is used. **WARNING!** If you have a newer version of Microsoft Excel with the XLStart feature enabled, you may have conflicts when trying to link Student Records to Excel.

Network Student Data

You must have a local area network (LAN) in order to network student data across computers. Networking student data will allow teachers and students access to their work from any computer in the network.

WARNING! We recommend that you set up the network prior to beginning your school year. If you choose to set up the network after the school year has begun, you will have to manually transfer current student work and grades to the network. For technical support, visit our web site at:

www.aop.com/HomeSchool/TechSupport/

To set up the network:

Step 1 – Teacher's Computer:

1. Do a regular install on the teacher's computer. Install all the subjects.
2. Share the SOS directory. (Right-click on the folder marked SOS | go to properties | select the Sharing tab | Choose Shared As | Choose Access Type as full.)

Step 2 – Each Student's Computer:

1. Map a new drive and link it to the shared directory (folder) on the teacher's computer. (Double-click on My Computer | Click on Map Drive on the toolbar;

the Map Network Drive will pop up | Choose a drive that is not in use | Type in the path to the shared file on the teacher's computer (i.e. \\name of teacher's computer\name of shared file, which is usually **sos**) | Select "Reconnect at logon."

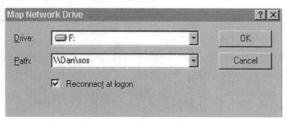

2. Insert any subject CD-ROM (the "A" disk of any multi-CD set) into the CD drive and run the install.exe program. Select "Install Student on Network" and replace the line C:\sos\ with x:\ (where x is the new drive you just mapped; see picture below.)

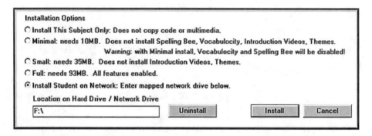

Note: You do not have to install all the subjects on student computers since students will be accessing the program from the teacher's computer where you have already installed all the subjects.

Note: You cannot copy the information from the CD-ROMs to a hard drive. Students must have the CD-ROMs when they are working on their school lessons.

Step 3 – Student and School Setup

Follow the standard procedures for setting up your school and your students as outlined in Setting Up. The only additional step you need to take in School Setup is to select the box labeled Network Student Data. Enabling this feature sets up a lock-out system that gives warnings when students and teachers are accessing information at the same time (i.e. going into the same lesson at the same time).

Chapter 2

ORIENTATION

Read through this section to learn the basics of being a teacher or a student in Switched-On Schoolhouse.

This brief orientation will help you get started in the Switched-On Schoolhouse by explaining what you can do in the program. By reading this section, you will more readily understand the step-by-step instructions found in later chapters.

TEACHER ORIENTATION

Switched-On Schoolhouse is your curriculum, teacher handbook, answer key, and grading book all wrapped up in one educational learning system.

If you are new to the Schoolhouse you will find the first few weeks to be a period of adjustment to computerized education. This is to be expected, but before long you will be sailing through the various menus and pinpointing the areas where your students need your help the most. The computer is not meant to replace you, rather to save you time by taking care of administrative tasks and simple grading.

Getting Organized

Switched-On Schoolhouse is designed to give you the flexibility to make important, education-related decisions as you see fit. The following is a summary of some of the available options and a list of suggestions for using them.

Lesson Plans. The lesson plan is a guide to keep you on track throughout the year. It is based on the calendar you have set up and the subjects you have assigned. If you go on an unexpected vacation, or your student gets ill, you can make changes to the calendar and print out a new lesson plan. You can also use this lesson plan for your student's records.

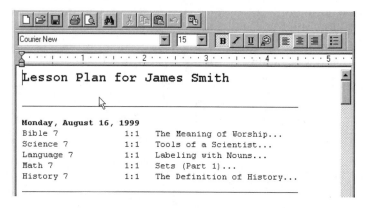

Subjects are divided into units, lessons, quizzes, tests, and projects. A subject can have 5–11 units (most have 10 units). The units are then divided into a number of lessons and projects. Each unit also has 2–5 quizzes and a final unit test. The lesson plan uses this structure to divide the work evenly over the school year, based on the number of questions in the lessons.

Customizing the Program. There are many ways for you to customize the program in School Setup and Student Setup. The program settings influence how the student learns and performs in Switched-On Schoolhouse.

Focus Learning System. The default settings create an environment that encourages students to stick with a lesson until all their answers are correct. Students will be placed in a mastery loop called "Focus Learning" which returns them to all incorrect lesson problems until all are answered correctly. (See *School Setup* and *Student Setup*.)

The default program settings disable Focus Learning during quizzes and tests. Students answer questions one at a time and only get one attempt at answering. Once they leave a quiz or test, they cannot return and all unanswered questions are graded as 0 points. This form of testing prohibits students from guessing answers by use of context clues gleaned from other questions, providing a good measure of a student's knowledge. The teacher has the option to disable Focus Learning and make the quizzes and tests Open Page (students can loop through until they are done) and Open Book (students can enter and exit at will).

The Focus Learning System:

- Acts as an automatic, self-adjusting lesson plan.
- Creates an environment for efficient learning.
- Concentrates on students' weak areas.
- Acts as a built-in tutor.

Preview Work. You can look over the curriculum ahead of time so you know what your student will be doing. You can choose to skip over lessons, skip over questions, or re-arrange units if you want your student to learn the topics in a different order. You can also set up a block to stop the student from racing ahead. (See *Unit Grades Menu*.)

Teacher Tip: Go before the students and block all the quizzes and tests. That way, your students must let you know when it is time for a quiz or test. You can then check their work to make sure they are ready for the test.

Add Your Own Project. Each unit has a lesson called "Special Project." This lesson is available for you to create your own assignment and incorporate it into the grading. You can use this space for field trip reports, book reports, or current-events projects (see *Unit Grades Menu.*)

Assign or Skip Projects. Default program settings assign certain projects and skip others. You can change these settings with the click of a button. Click on the project bar to preview the project before assigning or skipping. (See *Unit Grades Menu*).

Create a Custom Subject. You can combine any subjects across any grade levels and rearrange units. For example, say your 7th grade math student is missing some key concepts from 6th grade. You can create a custom subject by taking 2 units from 6th grade and adding those to the beginning of his 7th grade math. The automatic lesson plan will then spread that work out over the course of the school year so that he finishes all of it within the year and has caught up on what he was missing (see *Unit Grades Menu*).

Set Theme. You and your students can change the "look and feel" of your personal desktops by choosing a theme (wooddesk, pastel, sand, etc.). The theme chosen in Teacher Mode will display on the front Student Menu.

Day-to-Day

Handling student questions. Your students will probably have questions as they progresses through the material. If you are on hand to field questions, you can pop into Teacher Mode to look at the Answer Key. Your experience and the Teacher Mode answer key should be sufficient to answer all immediate student questions.

Teacher Tip: The toolbar controls have matching keyboard controls. For example, pressing the F2 key is the same as clicking on NEXT. F3 is the same as the UTIL. See *Controls* in Chapter I for more keyboard controls.

If you are not available to field questions, students can skip a troublesome problem by sending you a note and sending the problem to you. There will be a "?" in the score box when the problem gets sent to you. As you grade work, you can type a note in reply and send the problem back to the student. This option can be turned off in Student Setup.

Messages from the student are indicated by a flashing "Message" notice located near the problem number. To read the message, click on the little notepad located beside the problem number.

Teacher Tip: Concepts build upon each other, especially in Mathematics and Language Arts. When you are helping your students learn a new concept, you may have to review the basics with them before they can fully grasp new content. If necessary you can go back and clear an entire lesson for the student to repeat.

Grading. You will want to follow behind the student to grade essays and paragraphs and read any messages he or she has left for you. In Teacher Mode, Grading Menu, the "Needs Grading" icon appears on a subject notifying you that problems need your grading and/or attention. Click on that notice to go directly to the problems needing attention. The answer key for paragraph-type problems is displayed below the paragraph box. The answer key for computer-graded problems can be seen by clicking on KEY on the toolbar; the answer key will temporarily replace student answers. Type a grade in the score box. See *Grading* for more information.

Teacher Tip: Even if there is no "Needs Grading" notice, use the Unit Grades Menu to look through the lessons, paying particular attention to incorrectly-answered problems. These will be colored red so you can quickly spot them.

Teacher Tip: If you disagree with a grade, you can click on the score box and change the score. For example, the student might spell a word so that the program does not recognize it as being the correct answer. You override the grade by giving partial or full credit. If a student is not using the Focus Learning mode and has done poorly in a lesson, you can "clear" that lesson and send it back for the student to re-do (see *Unit Grades Menu*).

You can also set up a "Study Student" for the student to practice his or her lessons on before taking a quiz or test. Simply add another student and assign the same subjects, skipping over the lessons that are not needed for review.

Note: You will want to "block" all the quizzes and tests so the student doesn't practice on those before taking the real ones!

Backups. Get into the habit of keeping regular backups of your student's work. Students can even back up their own work through the back up button on the Student Menu.

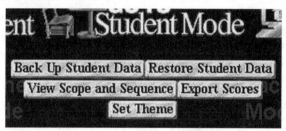

Activities Away From the Computer

Special Projects. Each unit has a lesson called "Special Project." This lesson is available for you to create your own assignment and incorporate it into the grading. You can use this space to assign extra projects like models or map work done away from the computer.

Experiments. Science experiments are demonstrated for the student through video clips, but there's nothing like hands-on learning. The required materials and procedures are listed so you can repeat the experiments at home. (Go to the Reference section of the first unit to print out the list of materials needed for the entire course.)

Novels. Language Arts 9, 10, 11, and 12 come with paperback novel(s). Unit lessons on the computer guide students in their reading and comprehension of the material.

Research. To meet project requirements, students

may need to go on field trips to the library or a museum, or have access to other outside reference sources for their research.

Printing Lessons. Printing the lessons is useful when you are juggling multiple students on one computer. In Teacher Mode you can print screen shots or just the plain text of the lessons. Students can use these printed sheets to study from as they prepare for quizzes.

Print Vocabulary/Spelling Word Lists. In Teacher Mode you can go into the curriculum and print the vocabulary and spelling word lists. Students can use these to study the definitions and to learn their spelling away from the computer.

Study. Encourage students, especially those in high school to take notes. Note-taking is an important skill that they will need for college. They can then use their notes to study while they are away from the computer.

Practice Skills. Take advantage of opportunities to make practical application of what the student is studying. For example, if the student is studying about measurements, move into the kitchen and bake some cookies. If the student is studying about plants, grow an indoor garden. Be creative and get involved in what your students are learning.

Teaching Tips

The following are some subject-specific tips from our editors.

Bible

Students will be able to answer the majority of questions in the lessons without reading the suggested Scripture passages. Encourage your students to read the verses anyway to get the proper context.

Switched-On Schoolhouse uses the King James Version for the Scripture references. When the sentence structure of a passage is similar in other versions, we have added modern English answers to the answer key as well.

Memory verses (if any) are reviewed in the Reference section of each unit.

College Planner

College planning is a family project. Parents should participate in the process with their student. There's even a lesson in Unit 4 (Financial Aid) called *A Message to Parents (and Students)*.

Health Quest

Health Quest is a one-semester, five-unit course. If you use a 180-day calendar, the lesson plan will spread the course out over the entire school year. If you would like your student to finish Health Quest in one semester, either create a semester calendar for this subject or ignore the lesson plan.

Health Quest contains numerous teacher-graded projects which can be completed "off the work track." This advantage quickly becomes a burden to both student and teacher if projects are allowed to pile up. As with all schoolwork, projects should be completed as assigned, in a timely manner.

History and Geography

Use the "Special Projects" feature to add current-events projects to the student's studies. Ideas range from participating in community events to reading recent newspaper or magazine articles. The project page can be used for summaries and/or reports based on such readings.

For geography, students can do mapping activities. Make them personal. For example, if a family member is traveling on business, or a relative is visiting from out of town, have the student map these trips to gain a better understanding of the physical world.

Language Arts

Language Arts includes rigorous capitalization and punctuation exercises. Many of these use pre-loaded text boxes requiring multiple answers. Because the program treats a multiple-answer response inside a single text box as one answer, you may want to consider overriding the grade generated by the program. For example, a five-answer response within a single textbox would receive a zero if any one of the five answers were wrong. You would want to manually change that grade to an 80% if the answers were to be equally weighted.

Use the "Special Project" in each unit to assign book reports using on-line e-texts or books from your local library.

Mathematics

Math is a step-by-step process. Research shows that the majority of students do not like to work step-by-step. Sometimes, when a student sees the answer to a problem, he or she skips steps to enter the answer. Math rewards careful, deliberate work.

It is important for your student to fill in all the steps of a problem. If your student enters a correct answer and the program grades it as incorrect, it could be that an intermediate step was not entered or was entered incorrectly. The computer generally considers these steps in the grading. It is also important to use the model in the text as a guide. Often, there is more than one way to solve a problem. To help everyone, problems are generally scripted to follow the model.

Science

Science experiments are demonstrated for the student through video clips, illustrating the steps for you to follow on your own. The required materials and procedures are listed so you can repeat the experiments at home. (Go to the Reference section of the first unit to print out the list of materials needed for the entire course.) Also, note that there are many extra experiments that you can assign to your young scientist.

Spanish

If students really want to speak, listen, read, and write in Spanish, they must study every day. In the lessons, students are asked to write, discuss, see, listen, and speak in Spanish. In addition to regular lessons, Internet activities are given in the lessons, allowing students to explore the virtual Spanish world. Another way to expose students to Spanish is to plan a vacation, a mission trip, or an outreach to a Spanish-speaking area.

State History

State History is actually a series of 13 research projects. Students have a wonderful oppor-tunity to work on their research and writing skills while learning about their state. Each project contains a multimedia-enhanced lesson and directions for completion.

When you assign State History to your student, he or she will immediately be sent all 13 projects. Although the State History icon appears on the Schoolwork page, all the work is accessed from the project assignment icons.

State History is a one-semester course. When you use a 180-day calendar to create the lesson plans, State History will be spread evenly throughout the entire school year. The lesson plan will "assign" a new project approximately every 14 days. Keep in mind that although all the projects will appear on the student's desktop all at once, they will be due at different times. If you would like your student to complete State History in one semester, you should either create a semester calendar for this subject or ignore the lesson plan.

Help File

If you ever need more instructions on how to perform an activity in Switched-On Schoolhouse, click HELP on your toolbar. The Help file is "context sensitive" which means it will open to the page that matches what you are working on. For example, if you are in Student Setup and click on HELP, the Help file will open to the explanation of Student Setup.

To search for a topic in the Help file, click on **Search.** In the Index tab, type in a keyword, for example, "Printing." Highlight the index entry you want, then click Display. If the keyword is found on more than one page, choose the page you want, then click Display. Scroll down the help page to find your topic.

STUDENT ORIENTATION

If this is your first year with Switched-On Schoolhouse, there are a few things that you need to learn about doing your schoolwork on the computer before you begin your studies.

Getting Started

Double-click on the light-switch icon on your desktop to enter the Schoolhouse. If you have an icon set up just for you, you will go directly to your Schoolwork Menu. If all the students and the teacher are using the same icon you will have to look for your name in the opening menu, the Student Menu.

Click on your name and type in your password (if your teacher gave you one) to get to your Schoolwork Menu.

The Schoolwork Menu displays the subjects you are studying and posts your grades. To start working, click on a subject icon near the top of the screen. You must have that subject's CD-ROM in your CD drive to access your lessons.

Note: If you do not have any subjects assigned yet, tell your teacher.

Daily Lessons

Each of your subjects are divided into units, lessons, quizzes, tests, and projects. A subject can have 5–11 units (most have 10 units). The units are then divided into a number of lessons and projects. Each unit also has 2-5 quizzes and a final unit test. The lessons always start off with text information for you to read followed by problems for you to answer.

Message boxes. A teacher-student message box appears every time you go into a subject. This box provides a place for you and your teacher to send each other questions, answers, and announcements. Click on **Start Lesson** at the top of the message box to begin your schoolwork.

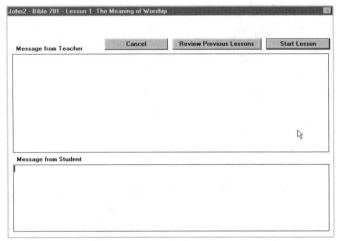

The message boxes are subject specific, meaning there is a different message box for each subject. The message boxes will only open when you are in the curriculum. You can access the message box by clicking on a subject icon, or, while you are in a lesson, by pressing the Pause key, by holding down the CTRL key and pressing M on the keyboard, or by clicking on UTIL (toolbar) then choosing Messages (for your subject name and grade level).

Multimedia. As you read through your lessons you'll find a variety of multimedia items to click on. Look for words colored blue, tiny video-recorder and speaker symbols on pictures, and the instructions to "click here." When your mouse pointer turns into a little hand, click to see what happens. Some presentations you click on will play on their own (videos), but for other presentations, you will have to click through at your own pace (slide shows).

Lesson Problems. When you finish reading a lesson, click on NEXT on your toolbar or press the F2 key on your keyboard. The first problem pops up at the bottom of the screen. Answer the problem and then click NEXT. Your answer will be graded immediately. A correct answer brings up the next problem. An incorrect answer leaves the problem on the screen so you can take another look at it. Sometimes you will even be shown a "hint" about the correct answer to the problem. When you get a problem wrong, the background screen displays "Incorrect: Click Next to Continue."

You cannot change the answer at this point. Click NEXT to move on.

If you need help in figuring out how to use the computer to answer a question or solve a problem, click on the HELP button on your toolbar for an explanation.

Student Tip: Learn to use the keyboard and mouse shortcuts! Instead of clicking NEXT on the toolbar, you can press the F2 key on your keyboard or you can right-click with the mouse. To learn more keyboard controls see *Controls* in Chapter 1.

Spelling. Spelling counts in fill-in-the-blank questions (short answers). Words that are only "close to" the correct spelling will get points taken off or may be marked completely wrong.

Focus Learning. If Focus Learning is in operation, you will get another chance to answer the lesson problems you get wrong. When you get to the end of the lesson, you will loop back to any incorrectly answered problems and answer them again. When your lesson is complete (all answers are correct), the message box pops up again. You can "Cancel" to go back to your Schoolwork Menu; "Review Previous Lesson" if you want to study what you've already done; "Start Lesson" if you want to continue.

I'm stuck! If you are having trouble with a question and your teacher is available, you can use the Problem Helps found in the UTIL button on the toolbar. Click on UTIL and choose from the options of "Give-up" (get a score of zero), Skip (go past), or Answers (see answer). Your teacher will then have to type in the Teacher Password for the program to accept your choice.

If your teacher isn't available right away, you can leave a note and move on. Click on the small notepad near the problem number. Type in a message explaining the trouble you are having and then click on "Leave message for teacher; skip problem." The problem will then be sent to the teacher, and you will be able to continue on with your work. If your teacher has turned off this feature, you will not be able to skip the problem.

Grading

Your teacher grades all paragraph answers and projects. Your teacher may also change the grades on any computer-graded problems. Your grades are not final until your teacher, not the computer, says they are final.

Work sent back. Sometimes you will find yourself automatically put back into a lesson that you thought you had finished! Your teacher, who is following behind you, grading and answering your messages, has changed something and wants you to see it. You might have to redo some work. Check in the flashing message box to see what your teacher wants you to do. If there is no message, redo the problem, and go on.

Grades. The grades for all your subjects are displayed on the buttons at the bottom of the Schoolwork Menu. Each unit is represented by a button. Click on a unit button to see the unit's table of contents and the grades for each of the lessons (i.e., the Review Menu). Click on a lesson to see the grades for each of the problems.

Studying for Quizzes and Tests

Each time you go into a new lesson, the message box pops up giving the option to "Review Previous Lesson." Click this button to go to the Review Menu. The Review Menu is a table of contents listing all your lessons and projects for the unit. Click on a lesson title to see the lesson. You can scroll through the entire lesson and see all the problems. To see the answer key, click on Key on the toolbar or hold down the Shift key on your keyboard.

You can also get to the Review Menu through the Review buttons on your Schoolwork Menu. Each subject has a row of 5 to 11 buttons that link directly to the "table of contents" for each unit.

Note: You can only go into the lessons you have finished. You can't change the answers.

Quizzes and Tests

There are three different styles of quizzes and tests available in Switched-On Schoolhouse. Your teacher decides which kind to give you.

1. **Default setting.** The quiz feeds you one problem at a time, just like in the lessons, but you will only get **one chance** to answer the problem. You will not loop back to the beginning of the quiz. Problems will be graded as you complete them. In this mode, make sure you have given your FINAL answer before you click NEXT. Once you leave the quiz or test, you cannot go back in. All unanswered questions will be graded as "0" points.

2. **Open Page.** In an open page quiz, you will still get one question at a time, but you will be able to continuously loop through the questions until you click DONE. Nothing will be graded until you click DONE. Once you leave the quiz or test you cannot go back in. All unanswered questions will be graded as "0" points.

3. **Open Book.** Like "Open Page," Open Book quizzes allow you to continuously cycle through the problems until you click DONE. You will also be able to exit or enter the quiz or test at will. All unanswered questions will be graded as "0" points.

Student Tip: Study before you take a quiz or test. Even if you scored 100% on all your lessons you still need to study. You can study your lessons by clicking on "Review Previous Lesson" as discussed above or through the grade grid buttons at the bottom of your Schoolwork Menu. The Review Menu shows you the table of contents of each unit and lets you see work that you have finished.

Projects

Project icons will pop up on your Schoolwork Menu throughout the year. These may be Science experiments, essays, or other projects. Click on a project icon to view the assignment. You can go in and out of a project until you click on the button "Check here when your project is complete" at the top of the instructions page. Clicking this button sends the project to your teacher.

Generally, you will use a word processor to complete projects. Click on the Report icon to open a word processor. The projects automatically link to WordPad. (If you have another word processor, your teacher can link the projects to that word processor instead.) When you save your work, do NOT change the name of the project. Click Save NOT Save as.

Utilities

Click on UTIL on the toolbar to bring up Utility Functions. You may choose from the list of programs to which your teacher has created links in School Setup. All subjects have their own Reference page and message box. You must be in Review mode (looking at lessons you have finished) to use Autohightlight. Printing options work only in Teacher Mode.

When you click on UTIL, this box will open:

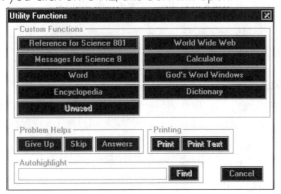

Reference

Each unit has its own Reference section. Here you will find all your vocabulary words, web links, and videos listed for that unit. The reference sections may also contain formulas, memory verses, or other information depending on the subject. To access the Reference section, click on UTIL on your toolbar or go to the Review Menu.

STUDY TIPS

Autohightlight. While in any lesson, quiz, test, or project in Review Mode you can use "Autohighlight" in the utilities box to find a topic you want to study. Click on UTIL on the toolbar. Type in a word or phrase in the Autohighlight box and click Find. All instances of the word or phrase you typed will be highlighted for you.

Note-taking. Another way you can study is to take notes from the lessons. Write down the important ideas, patterns, and formulas. Find a method of note-taking that works for you. Your teacher can help you with this.

"Pre-test." If you don't mind doing work over again, ask your teacher to clear a lesson for you to redo. Study first, then see if you can go through the lesson and answer all the questions without looking at the text for answers. You can also ask your teacher to set up a "Study Student" so you can do the lessons over again without deleting your real work.

Review. After completing a lesson, go back over it in Review Mode. (You are given the option to "Review Previous Lesson" in the message box that pops up before you begin work in a new lesson.) Skim over the text and look at your answers to the problems. Click on KEY on the toolbar to compare your answers with the answer key. If you don't quite understand the lesson material, go back over it. Ask your teacher to review it with you.

Practice. Make sure you practice each new skill you learn. If you are studying Spanish, practice your pronunciation. If you are learning calculus, do extra problems. Many of the Web links in Switched-On Schoolhouse will lead you to Web sites that will give you extra practice. Use these sites.

HELP FILE

If you ever get stuck, click on HELP on your toolbar. The Help file is "context sensitive" which means it will open to the page that matches what you are working on. For example, if you come to a drag-and-drop problem and you do not know what to do, click on HELP and the Help file will open the explanation of "Drag-and-Drop."

Chapter 3

TEACHER MODE

*Use the functions in
Teacher Mode to customize
Switched-On Schoolhouse.*

Setup and grading options in Teacher Mode allow
teachers some control over the learning process.
Among many options, teachers can restructure the
curriculum, set learning pace, and modify the grading
scale. Program default settings are merely a starting
point.

TEACHER MENU

To enter the teacher menu click on Go To Teacher
Mode. The Teacher Menu displays the class list with the
student names labeled on icons. We recommend that
teachers set up a password to restrict access to the
Teacher Menus. From this menu teachers can do the
following:

1. Add a Student.

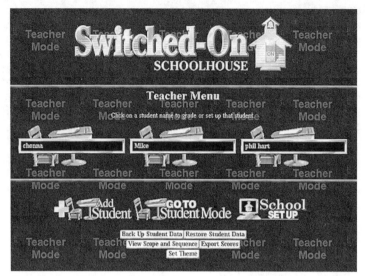

2. Go to Student Mode.

3. Enter School Setup.

4. Back up/ Restore Data.

5. View Scope and Sequence.

6. Export Scores.

7. Set theme for the teacher's desktop.

Add/Delete a Student

1. Click on Go to Teacher Mode.

2. Click on the Add Student icon.

3. Type in the student's name and Click OK.

Note: To delete a student, hold down the shift key and click on the student's name while in the Teacher Menu. There is also a button to delete a student in Student Setup.

Back Up/Restore Student Data

Click to back up your student's work (see *Backups* on p.24). Click to replace your student's work with the files you backed up (see *Restore* on p.26).

View Scope and Sequence

The Scope and Sequence displays a detailed list of subject unit and lesson titles available in Switched-On Schoolhouse.

1. Go to Teacher Mode.
2. Click on View Scope and Sequence.
3. Choose the grade level to see the detailed listing of all the available subjects.

Export Scores

Export scores to create a report on student grades. Once the data has been exported, you can import the scores into a spreadsheet or word-processing program where you can arrange it into tables. The information is set up using tabs and includes the student names, lesson titles, and grades as follows:

ID Name Subject Unit Type Score Lesson

ID= Student number
Name= Student name
Subject= academic subject
Unit= unit number (1–11)
Type= one of the following: L=lesson, Q=Quiz, T=Test, P=Project, !=Student (total score), U=Unit (for unit score), S=Subject (for subject score)
Score= grade value
Lesson= lesson name and number
#= number of activity (counts lessons, quizzes, tests, and projects).

To export scores:

1. Click on Go to Teacher Mode.

2. Click on Export Scores.

3. Choose the location where you want to export the scores to and select OK.

4. Scores will be exported as a .txt file called "scores.txt." You can then bring the data into your own programs to organize how you like. (See your manual for that particular program to learn how to import text with tabs.)

For example:

To convert the text into a table in Microsoft Word:

1. Highlight the text.

2. Pull down the Table menu.

3. Select "Convert text to table." The number of columns will be tabulated for you. You can change the size of the columns now or after the table has been made. Make sure the "Separate text at" option is set to tabs.

4. Click OK.

Note: This creates a large table that is better displayed as "landscape." To change the page layout to landscape, pull down the File menu, select Page Setup, select the Paper Size tab, and choose Landscape.

Set Theme for Desktop (Teacher)

The theme changes the look of the program.

1. Click on Go to Teacher Mode.

2. Click on Set Theme.

3. Choose your theme and select OK.

School Setup Menu

School Setup

Note: These are advanced functions, and Switched-On Schoolhouse will operate with the default settings.

Teacher Password

Grade Calculations

Grade required for A:	92 %
Grade required for B:	84 %
Grade required for C:	72 %
Grade required for D:	64 %
Spelling Penalty	15 %
Weight for Exercises	5
Weight for Projects	20
Weight for Quizzes	25
Weight for Tests	50

Display Letter Grades ☒

Display Percentage Grades ☒

Installation and Defaults

Install Subject From CD-ROM

Create Custom Subject for Use by All Students

Uninstall Subjects from School

Set Calendar for School for school year starting in 1999

☐ Allow Lesson Blocking

☐ Network Student Data

Program Locations

Locate Word Processor for Student (shift-click to auto-locate)

C:\PROGRA-1\ACCESS-1\wordpad.exe

Locate Word Processor for Teacher (shift-click to auto-locate)

C:\PROGRA-1\MICROS-1\OFFICE\winword.exe

Locate World Wide Web Browser (shift-click to auto-locate)

C:\PROGRA-1\INTERN-1\iexplore.exe

Utility Program Locations

Name:	Locate
Location:	
Name:	Locate
Location:	
Name:	Locate
Location:	
Name:	Locate
Location:	
Name:	Locate
Location:	
Name:	Locate
Location:	

Reset School Setup to Default State

Teachers can customize Switched-On Schoolhouse by resetting the options in School Setup. Changes are automatically saved and applied to all students when you click DONE.

The School Setup Menu contains:

- Teacher password.

- Grade calculations.
- Installation and defaults.
- Program locations
- Utility Program Locations

Teacher Password

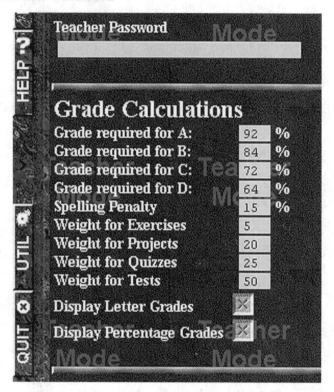

1. Click on Go to Teacher Mode.
2. Click on School Setup.
3. Type in a Teacher Password. The password restricts access to the Teacher Mode and enables the Problem Helps utility options. (The Problem Helps allow the teacher to access certain controls from Teacher Mode while in the student's lesson. For example, if the student has trouble answering a question and calls you over, you can go to the

Problem Helps on the UTIL button on the toolbar and choose "Answer" to see the answer for that question. You will then be prompted to enter your password. The three Problem Helps are: **Skip**, **Give Up**, or **Answers**.)

Note: If no password is entered, students can freely access Teacher Mode and the answer key. If you forget your password, you can access Teacher Mode by holding down the SHIFT key and clicking on the Go to Teacher Mode icon. This will delete the password and you can type in a new one. (Students: if you do this, your teacher will know!)

Grade Calculations

1. Click on Go to Teacher Mode.
2. Click on School Setup.
3. Customize the following:

Letter Grade Calculation

Change letter grade requirements by typing the percent required next to the letter grade. Default mode automatically sets the grades at: 92% = A, 84% = B, 72% = C, 64% = D.

Spelling Penalty

The teacher can set the percentage that will be taken off the students' scores for misspelled words. Default mode is set to 15%. However, this penalty does not apply to every word, since in some units, such as in Language Arts, the curriculum requires exact spelling and punctuation. To require exact spelling in all text, set spelling penalty to 100%.

Note: The spell check allows for certain phonetic combinations. Spelling errors outside these parameters will be marked incorrect. Default settings apply only to words of seven characters or more. To change the spelling setting to include shorter words, go to Student Setup and select "Easy spelling."

Relative Score Weighting for Lessons

Set the Relative Score Weighting for Lessons to determine the weighting of the students' total grades. In default mode the lesson exercises are set at 5%, projects are set at 20%, quizzes are set at 25% and tests are set at 50%. The weighting is based on percentages rather than total marks.

Grade Display

Set the grade display to **letter grades** and/or **percentage grades** to determine how the grades will be shown in students and teacher menus as well as printed grades.

Installation and Defaults

Install Subject from CD-ROM

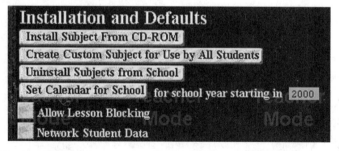

There are two ways to add subjects to Switched-On Schoolhouse: directly off the CD-ROM using the install.exe program or through School Setup. To install a subject through School Setup:

1. Click on Go to Teacher Mode.
2. Click on School Setup.

3. Click on Install Subject from CD-ROM.

4. Follow the on-screen instructions.

Create Custom Subjects

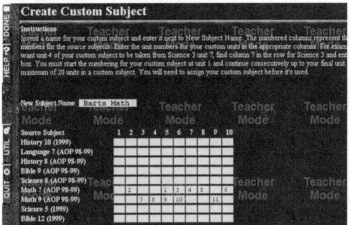

Teachers can create their own custom subjects by taking units from different subjects and/or reordering the units in a given subject. A customized subject can have up to 20 units. A custom subject can be created in School Setup for all students' use or in Student Setup for an individual student's use.

To create a custom subject for all students:

1. Click on Go to Teacher Mode.

2. Click on School Setup.

3. Click on Create Custom Subject.

4. Invent a new name for your custom subject and enter it next to New Subject Name.

5. As the graphic above shows, the numbered columns represent the unit numbers for the source subjects. Type numbers in the grid to indicate the order you want the units to be presented to the students. Number the units consecutively, starting with a "1." Do not repeat numbers. For example, if you want

the first unit of your custom subject to be taken from Language 8, unit 5, find the row for Language 8, go over to column 5 and enter a "I" in that box, and so on.

Note: When you create a custom subject, you are making a "shortcut" to the source subjects. In the SOS messaging system, the subject title will not be the custom subject name you made up (e.g., "My Language"), rather, it will be the name of the source subject. However, the custom subject name will appear on the subject bar.

The newly created custom subject will appear in the list of available subjects in Student Setup for each student.

Uninstall Subjects

1. Click on Go to Teacher Mode.
2. Click on School Setup
3. Click on Uninstall Subjects.
4. Select the subjects you want to remove. Click on DONE on the toolbar.

Note: Uninstalling a subject is not to be confused with unassigning a subject. **Uninstalling** a subject takes the subject completely off the system. **Unassigning** a subject is the equivalent of taking a student's book away for a short time (the student cannot access it until it is reassigned).

School Calendar

The calendar must be set up in order to create a lesson plan. There are two types of calendars: one for the school and one for every student (see *Student Setup*). When created first, the school calendar can be used in creating lesson plans for each student.

Note: Any changes made to an individual student calendar will override the school calendar for that specific student only.

To set up the school calendar:

1. Click on Go to Teacher Mode.

2. Click on School Setup.

3. Click on Set Calendar for School. (Type in the starting date for the school year if you need to.)

4. Select all the school days from the beginning to the end of the school year. To deselect a day, click on the indented box.

5. Click on DONE to save.

Note: The program sets the calendar default at 2001; however you can enter any year from 2000 to 2010 and still be able to use the Load Default Calendar option. For any year you enter, the resulting calendar page will post a twenty-four month menu of calendars beginning in January of your year of choice.

Load Default 180-day School Year automatically selects a standardized, nine-month school year running from late August to May. If you decide to use this calendar, you can still modify any days to fit into your school's schedule. Simply click on a day to select or deselect it. Click DONE to save the changes.

Note: If you change the calendar after lesson plans have been created, you will have to go to Student Setup for each student to make new lesson plans.

Changing or Clearing the Calendar

To change or clear a school calendar:

1. Click on Go to Teacher Mode.
2. Click on School Setup.
3. Click on Set Calendar.
4. Adjust the calendar by selecting or deselecting the appropriate days.
5. To erase the entire calendar, click on Clear Calendar.
6. To go to the default calendar, click on Load Default 180-day School Year.

Allow Lesson Blocking

Select this option if you want to set up "road blocks" to keep your student from racing ahead. Once Lesson Blocking is enabled, you can go into the Unit Grades Menu change the "Assigned" buttons to "Blocked." Students will have to wait for the teacher to assign the blocked lesson before they proceed. (Example: Block the quizzes and tests so you can make sure all student work is graded before they take the quiz or test.)

Network Student Data

Select this option when sharing student data across networked computers on a Local Area Network. Enabling this feature sets up a lock-out system that gives warnings when teachers and students are accessing information at the same time. See *Advanced Setup*.

Program Locations

When you install the program, Switched-On Schoolhouse automatically finds and links to your word processing programs and World-Wide Web browser. Students will be linked to WordPad. Teachers will be linked to Microsoft Word if Word is installed on the hard drive. If you do not have Microsoft Word, the

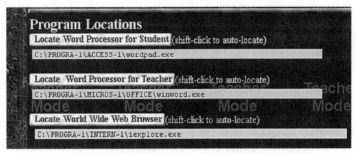

Program Locations

Locate Word Processor for Student (shift-click to auto-locate)

C:\PROGRA~1\ACCESS~1\wordpad.exe

Locate Word Processor for Teacher (shift-click to auto-locate)

C:\PROGRA~1\MICROS~1\OFFICE\winword.exe

Locate World Wide Web Browser (shift-click to auto-locate)

C:\PROGRA~1\INTERN~1\iexplore.exe

teacher's word processor will be linked to WordPad. If you would like to change the word processor or Web browser, follow the step-by-step instructions below.

To change the Word Processor or World-Wide Web Browser:

1. Click on Go to Teacher Mode.

2. Click on School Setup.

3. Click on Locate to find the program you want, or shift-click on Locate to have Switched-On Schoolhouse find the program for you. Auto-locate looks in order for: word.exe, winword.exe, then WordPad.exe for the word processor. For the Web browser auto-locate looks for iexplorer.exe, nsgold.exe, then netscape.exe. (**Note:** Auto-locate may take a few minutes to find your program).

4. If you need to locate the program yourself, you have to find the executable (.exe) file on your hard drive for the program you want. Programs you have installed onto your computer are usually located in C:\progra~1. Double-click on the folders on the right of the dialog box to see the contents on the left.

5. Choose the program you want by double-clicking on it, or by clicking on it once then selecting OK. The location will be copied automatically into the "Location" line in School Setup.

Notes:

1. Your word processor must work in rich text format.

2. You must have Internet access in order for your students to visit the World-Wide Web through the curriculum. Students can access the Internet browser through the UTIL button on the toolbar or can link directly to specific web pages via the WWW links in the lessons.

Utility Programs

Through Switched-On Schoolhouse you can connect up to six reference programs from your computer. Students can access them from the UTIL button on the toolbar.

The basic procedure is the same to add all links:

1. Go to Teacher Mode.

2. Click on School Setup.

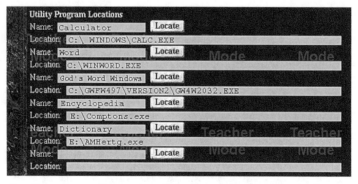

3. Enter a name to describe the program to which you are making a link. This name will appear as a button in the Utility box for the student to click on.

4. Click on Locate.

5. Find the executable (.exe) file on your hard drive for the program you want. Typically, you will need to look in C:\Windows for accessory programs like the

calculator (calc.exe). Other programs are usually located in C:\Program Files. Double-click on the folders on the right to see the contents on the left.

6. Choose the program you want by double-clicking on it, or by clicking on it once then selecting OK. The location will automatically be copied into the "Location" line in School Setup.

If you already know the location of the program, you can skip these steps and type directly into the box. Given the example entries in the graphic on the previous page, the resulting "Custom Functions" buttons (under the UTIL function) would display like this:

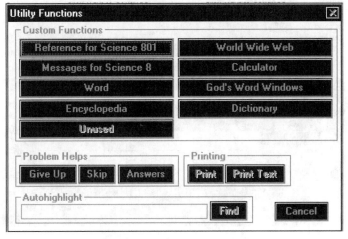

Reset to Default State

To Reset School Setup to Default State (back to the original default settings):

1. Go to **Teacher Mode**.
2. Click on School Setup.
3. Click on Reset School Setup to Default State. (**Note:** This will not affect the subjects or calendar.)

GRADING MENU

In Teacher Mode, the Grading Menu is displayed when a teacher clicks on a student's name. This menu shows the individual student's subjects, assigned projects, grades, "Needs Grading" notices, and "Past-due" notices.

Grading to Do

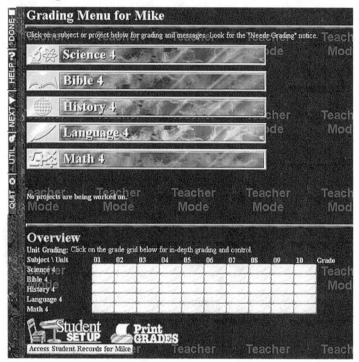

Assigned subjects are listed at the top of the screen. If a subject has a "Needs Grading" notice attached to it, then there are one or more problems in the subject that need to be graded and/or looked at by the teacher. Only completed lessons will display the "Needs Grading" notice

To grade a student's work:

1. Go to Teacher Mode.
2. Click on student's name.

3. Click on any subject icon with the "Needs Grading" notice to go to the first problem requiring grading for that subject.

4. Type the grade in the score box, then click NEXT on the toolbar to advance to the next problem requiring grading. (Grading options are outlined in detail in Chapter 4– Grading.)

5. For in-depth grading, click on the Unit Grade grid (Overview buttons) to see all lessons.

If Automatic Lesson Plans have been set up, then you may also see a "Past Due" notice on a subject. This indicates that the student is behind in his work according to pace set in the lesson plan.

Project Status

Project bars are displayed below the subjects after the student has marked a project as "completed." The screen will either indicate "No projects are being worked on" or will list by subject name, number, and title, the projects that have been assigned. For example, *Essay L505B–Making Conversation* is an essay called "Making Conversation" assigned from 5th grade Language Arts, unit 5, the second essay (B). Click on the project to grade it.

Note: The project icon will not appear in the teacher's Grading Menu until the teacher has graded past the lesson preceding the project assignment.

Overview

The following options are available under the "Overview" section of the Grading Menu.

Unit Grading

The final grades for each unit are listed in the grade grid near the bottom of the Grading Menu. For in-depth grading and control, click on a unit in the grade grid to open the Unit Grades Menu and view the student's work for that unit. (The Unit Grades Menu is explained later in this chapter, and grading options are outlined in detail in the next chapter.)

Print Grades

To print grades:

1. Click on Go to Teacher Mode.
2. Click on student's name.
3. Click on the Print Grades icon and click OK in the print menu which appears.

Access Student Records

Click on the Access Student Records button at the bottom of the Grading Menu to open a word processor document (uses the teacher's word processor program set up in School Setup). Here you can record additional information about your student. Students do not have access to this file; it is for administrative use only. See *Advanced Setup* for steps to customize this feature for a different program, such as a spreadsheet.

Student Setup Icon

The Student Setup icon links you to the Student Setup Menu. This menu is explained below.

STUDENT SETUP

The teacher can use the Student Setup Menu to customize the program for each student. Access the menu by clicking on the Student Setup icon in the

Grading Menu or go directly to Student Setup from the Teacher Menu by holding down the CTRL key and clicking on the student's name.

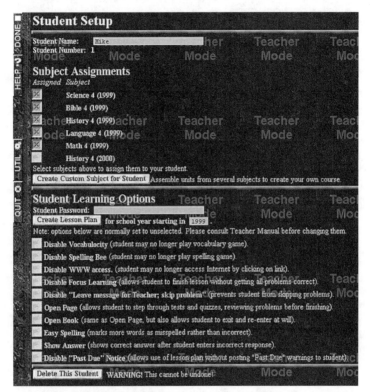

Student Name

To change a student's name on the icon:

1. Click on Go to Teacher Mode.

2. Click on student's name.

3. Click on Student Setup.

4. Type correct name beside "Student Name."

5. Click DONE on the toolbar to save the change.

Student Number

Student numbers are automatically assigned in the order the students are added. Students keep these numbers even when other students are deleted, changing the total number of students. You may need to know the student number when you do student backups and restore any lost data.

Subject Assignments

1. Go to Teacher Mode.
2. Click on student's name.
3. Click on Student Setup.
4. Click on the boxes next to the subjects you want the student to access. The box for an assigned subject is indented with an "X."

To unassign a subject so that a student cannot access it, click on the box under the "Assigned Subject" heading; the box will pop out and the "X" will disappear. This disables the subject, and the subject bar will not appear on the student's Schoolwork Menu. **Note:** Unassigning a subject does **not** delete the student's work. The work will re-appear when the subject is re-assigned.

Create Custom Subjects

Teachers can create a custom subject by taking units from different subjects and/or reordering the units in a given subject. A customized subject can have up to 20 units. A custom subject can be created in School Setup for all students to use or in Student Setup for an individual student's use. You may wish to refer to the Scope and Sequence to help you make decisions on which units to include. Keep in mind that you can jump across grade levels to help a student catch up on missed concepts.

To create a custom subject for an individual student:

1. Go to Teacher Mode.

2. Click on student's name.

3. Click on Student Setup.

4. Click on Create Custom Subject for Student.

5. Invent a name for your custom subject and enter it next to "New Subject Name."

6. The numbered columns represent the unit numbers for the source subjects. Type numbers (starting with 1) in the grid to indicate the order you want the units to be presented to the students. For example, if you want the first unit of your custom subject to be taken from Language 8, unit 5, find the row for Language 8, go to column 5, and enter a "1" in that box.

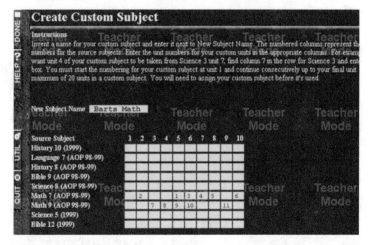

Note: Make sure you start with "1," number the units consecutively, and do not repeat numbers.

Remove Custom Subjects

To remove custom subjects from the individual student's menu:

1. Go to Teacher Mode.

2. Click on student's name.

3. Click on Student Setup.

4. Click on Remove Custom Subjects for Student (button appears only when there is a custom subject).

5. Select the subjects you want to remove.

6. Click on DONE on the toolbar. This deletes the custom subject; student work can still be accessed through the source subject.

Student Learning Options

Student Password. Type in a password to prevent students from accessing the work of other students. To change the password, erase and type in a new password.

Create Lesson Plan. The automatic Lesson Plan system generates a custom lesson plan for a student, using the student's assigned subjects and customized school year. The Automatic Lesson Plan produces a text file that can be printed and creates an internal system that generates the "Past Due" notices. The schoolwork for each subject is spread evenly over the year according to the total number of questions.

To create a lesson plan:

1. Go to Teacher Mode. (If you have not already done so, we recommend creating a School Calendar in School Setup for all the students.)

2. Click on a student's desk.

3. Click on Student Setup (If you have not already done so, Assign subjects to that student.)

4. Click on Create Lesson plan for school year starting in 2001 (change the date to 2000 if you are finishing off the 2000 school year.) The calendar for this particular student displays.

5. Choose Load Default 180-Day School Year to use the pre-programmed calendar or Use School Calendar to repeat the calendar you have previously set up in School Setup. Clear Calendar erases the calendar. The last option, Continue From Now can be used when you make changes to the calendar partway through the year and want to adjust the lesson plan. To select or deselect any single day, click on it.

6. Click DONE to save the changes and create the lesson plan. Follow the on-screen instructions.

View (and Print) Lesson Plan. To see the lesson plan and print out a copy, go to the Grading Menu (if you are in Student Set Up, click DONE to get to the Grading Menu.) and click on View Lesson Plan. To print, select the "File" menu then "Print." Students access their lesson plan from their Schoolwork Menu.

Lesson Plan Format (as seen in *View Lesson Plan*)

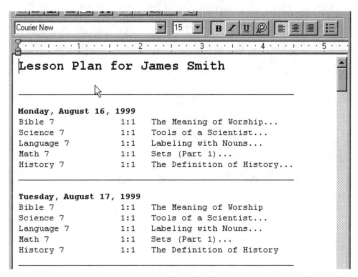

- The left column is the subject name.
- The middle column is the Unit Number : Lesson.

- The right column is the lesson name.
- A lesson "P" is a Project; "Q" is a Quiz; "T" is a Test.
- If "..." follows the name of the lesson, then that lesson continues to the next day.

WARNING! You cannot change the lesson plan by changing the text. Lesson plans are generated by Switched-On Schoolhouse using the assigned subjects and current calendar. Changing the text in WordPad or Notepad will have no effect on the lesson plan! You can change the lesson plan only by changing the calendar or the assigned subjects and clicking on Generate Lesson Plan again.

Once a Lesson Plan has been generated, the due date messages are posted and students will be warned by "Past Due" messages when they are falling behind. (To turn off the "Past Due" warnings, see *Learning Options* in *Student Setup*.)

Change the Lesson Plan. After changing the calendar or adding subjects, regenerate the lesson plan. Make sure only make sure you select the option Continue From Now at the top of the page.

When a student clicks on a subject bar, the due date will be printed in the message box along with the lesson title. When a student does not complete his assignment on time, a "Warning! Past Due!" notice will be posted on the subject bar and in the title on the message box. A student's Past Due notice is updated every time the teacher goes into the Grading Menu for that student (Past Due notices can be disabled in Student Setup.)

Clicking on Remove Lesson Plan will bring up the prompt, "This will erase the lesson plan for this student." Select OK or Cancel.

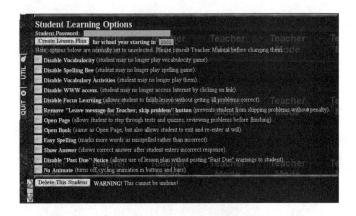

Student Learning Options
Student Password:
Create Lesson Plan for school year starting in 2001
Note: options below are normally set to unselected. Please consult Teacher Manual before changing them.
□ Disable Vocabulocity (student may no longer play vocabulocity game).
□ Disable Spelling Bee (student may no longer play spelling game).
□ Disable Vocabulary Activities (student may no longer play them).
□ Disable WWW access. (student may no longer access Internet by clicking on link).
□ Disable Focus Learning (allows student to finish lesson without getting all problems correct).
□ Remove "Leave message for Teacher; skip problem" button (prevents student from skipping problems without penalty).
□ Open Page (allows student to step through tests and quizzes, reviewing problems before finishing).
□ Open Book (same as Open Page, but also allows student to exit and re-enter at will).
□ Easy Spelling (marks more words as misspelled rather than incorrect).
□ Show Answer (shows correct answer after student enters incorrect response).
□ Disable "Past Due" Notice (allows use of lesson plan without posting "Past Due" warnings to student).
□ No Animate (turns off cycling animation in buttons and bars).
Delete This Student WARNING! This cannot be undone!

Disable Vocabulocity. Vocabulocity is a graphic-intense, 3D game created to challenge students to learn their vocabulary words and definitions. However, because it is so much fun, some students may spend too much time rescuing "Vocabulo City." The disable function allows teachers to turn off this feature. To see how much time your students are spending in Vocabulocity, go to the Unit Grades Menu for each student and look at the Vocabulocity statistics near the bottom of the menu.

Disable Spelling Bee. The Spelling Bee game is a fun way for students to practice spelling their vocabulary words in all subjects (except Spanish) and their spelling words in Language Arts. "Disable Spelling Bee" blocks students from playing the spelling game.

Disable Vocabulary Activities. Vocabulary Activities include any vocabulary drill games in addition to Vocabulocity and Spelling Bee. The new Vocabulary Activity for the 2001 version of Switched-On Schoolhouse is Alpha 14, the sequel to the original Vocabulocity. Select "Disable Vocabulary Activities" to remove Alpha 14 from the list of games that appear below each vocabulary (or spelling) list.

Disable WWW Access. Select the button to disable this student's World-Wide Web links. Student may no longer access the Internet through the WWW links or the UTIL button on the toolbar. If you have a student who spends too much time surfing the Web, you can disable his access and then turn it back on when his lessons are finished.

Disable Focus Learning. Disabling Focus Learning means the student will not have to get all answers correct in lessons before continuing on to the next lesson. See *Focus Learning*.

Disable "Leave message for teacher; skip problem". This function provides a way for students to break out of the mastery loop of Focus Learning. If students can't get an answer, they can click on the little notepad near the problem number to leave the teacher a message and skip the problem. This sends the problem to the teacher for review.

When this option is disabled, a student can no longer skip problems when leaving messages for the teacher.

Open Page. The Open Page option allows students to loop through quizzes and tests until they are finished; no grading is done until the student is completely finished. Any unworked problems will be given a zero. (**Note:** Students may be able to figure out answers based on clues found in other questions.)

Open Book. The Open Book option is the same as "Open Page," but also allows students to enter and exit the quiz or test at will until they indicate they are finished. (**Note:** Students will be able to go back to the lessons to find answers.)

Easy Spelling. The spelling penalty, set in Grade Calculations of Student Setup, counts a misspelled answer as correct, but takes points off for poor spelling. This spelling penalty works only for larger words, while shorter misspelled words are counted as completely wrong. However, when you select Easy Spelling, shorter misspelled words will also be marked correct (with points taken off for poor spelling). An even greater amount of spelling variations will be recognized and accepted in the larger words (i.e. when easy spelling is checked, students will get fewer fill-in-the-blank problems graded as "0" because of poor spelling.)

Show Answer, This option, when selected, shows students the correct answer after an incorrect response has been given. Students will still loop around in Focus Learning mode until they have entered in all answers correctly themselves.

Note: Some students may be tempted to loop through the lessons, looking at the answers instead of taking the time to work out the answers themselves.

Disable "Past Due" Notice. This option allows the use of lesson plans without posting "Past Due" warnings to the student when they fall behind. You may want to use this feature if you have manually edited the lesson plan so that it is different from the lesson plan the program is following. (**Note:** If you need to adjust the lesson plan, you can change the calendar and create a new lesson plan based on the changes. See *Lesson Plans.*)

Delete This Student. Click on Delete this Student to erase the student. This will erase all the student's work and grades and cannot be undone.

UNIT GRADES MENU

Unit Grades for:
LANGUAGE ARTS 501
JESUS, OUR EXAMPLE

Click on buttons below to grade Lessons.

1 The Author's Message	B:91%	Clear	Assigned
Project L501A-Finding the Topic		Clear	Assigned
2 Vowel Diphthong Design	A:100%	Clear	Assigned
Quiz 1	B:84%	Clear	Assigned
3 Spelling 1	A:100%	Clear	Assigned
Spelling Quiz 1	A:95%	Clear	Assigned
4 A Dialogue	A:100%	Clear	Assigned
5 Vocabulary Study	A:100%	Clear	Assigned
Quiz 2	B:90%	Clear	Assigned
6 Spelling 2	A:100%	Clear	Assigned
Spelling Project L501B-Story		Clear	Skipped
Spelling Quiz 2	A:100%	Clear	Assigned
7 Writing	A:100%	Clear	Assigned
Quiz 3	B:90%	Clear	Assigned
8 Spelling 3	A:100%	Clear	Assigned
Spelling Quiz 3	B:85%	Clear	Assigned
Special Project L501C		Clear	Skipped
TEST	A:93%	Clear	Assigned
Reference			

Similar to opening a textbook to the Table of Contents, clicking on a unit button in the Grading Menu opens up a content list: the Unit Grades Menu. This submenu displays the lesson grades and allows the teacher to take a closer look at the student's work. The Unit is divided into lessons, quizzes, projects, test, and reference.

Preview, Review, In-Depth Grading

To preview, review, or do in-depth grading:

1. Go to Teacher Mode.

2. Click on student's name.

3. Click on a subject/unit button located under the Overview title.

4. Click on a lesson title to go into the curriculum to preview, review, or grade.

84

5. Assign, skip, block, or clear work using the buttons to the right of the lesson titles (definitions follow)

Clear deletes all of the student's work and grades in a given lesson so the teacher can send the lesson back to the student for rework.

Assigned sets that lesson to be completed by the student. Most lessons start out as "Assigned."

Skipped closes the work to the student.

Blocked stops a student from going any further in the subject. ("Allow lesson blocking" must be selected in School Setup for this to work.)

Click on the Assigned, Skipped, or Blocked button to change the lesson status.

Assigning Extra and Special Projects

Switched-On Schoolhouse has extra projects that are initially Skipped (unassigned). The teacher can give a student additional work by assigning these projects.

1. Go to Teacher Mode.
2. Click on student's name.
3. Click on a subject/unit button located under the Overview title.
4. Click on the corresponding Skipped button to change it to Assigned. (You can click on the titles to preview the contents.)

Special Projects

To define a Special Project using your own instructions, follow steps 1 through 4 as shown above, then:

5. Click on the Special Project button to open the project.

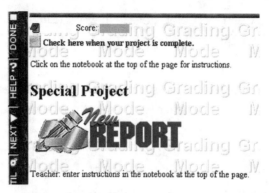

Score: ███████

Check here when your project is complete.

Click on the notebook at the top of the page for instructions.

Special Project

New **REPORT**

Teacher: enter instructions in the notebook at the top of the page.

6. Click on the small notepad found at the top left hand corner of the screen. A box will open up for you to type in the instructions for the assignment. This new project will be included in the overall grading system.

Status

The Unit Grades Menu also shows the following information underneath the list of lesson titles:

- when the student first began work in the unit
- when the student last worked in the unit
- total time spent in the unit
- time spent in the games Vocabulocity and Spelling Bee (number of tries, number of wins) **Note:** This information appears only when the student has used these features.

Chapter 4

GRADING

Grading is made easy in Switched-On Schoolhouse with automatic grading and built-in answer keys.

Switched-On Schoolhouse comes complete with a grading system that grades objective answers and automatically records the scores. Students know right away how well they are doing, and the teacher's grading workload is drastically reduced.

You will want to follow behind the student to grade essays and paragraphs and read any messages he or she has left for you. You will know there is grading to be done when the "Needs Grading" notice appears on the student's subject icons. Click on that notice to go directly to the problems needing attention.

The answer key for paragraph-type problems is displayed below the paragraph box. The answer key for computer-graded problems can be seen by clicking on KEY on the toolbar; the answer key will temporarily replace student answers. To grade any problem, type a grade in the score box next to the problem number.

Teacher Tip: Even if there is no "Needs Grading" notice, look through the lessons, paying particular attention to the problems the student got wrong. These will be colored red so you can quickly spot them.

AUTOMATIC GRADING

As soon as students click on NEXT (F2) while working in a lesson, the computer grades the answer. Correct answers are indicated with a verbal "That's correct!" "Good Answer!" or "That's the right answer!" and the next problem is given. Incorrect answers are indicated with a sound prompt, and the word "Incorrect" displays on the screen. The sound prompt depends upon the student's answer—completely wrong, misspelled, partially correct, or a grade of "A." To continue to the next problem or presentation, the student clicks on NEXT (F2).

See *Grade Calculations* for information on how to customize the grading and record keeping.

Teacher Tip: If you disagree with a problem grade, you can go into the lesson and change it. For example, the student might spell a word in such a way that the program does not recognize it as being the correct answer. You can override the computer and give partial or full credit.

TEACHER GRADING

To see if a subject needs grading:

1. Go to Teacher Mode.
2. Click on student's name.
3. Look for a "Needs Grading" notice on a subject icon.

4. Click on the icon to shortcut to the problem requiring teacher attention. You will either need to grade the problem, or answer a student's question about it. To grade, compare the student's answer with the suggested answer or marking guidelines (located below the paragraph box). Type the grade in the score box. To respond to a student's question, click on the notepad near the scorebox. Type in your response; then "clear" the scorebox by clicking in it and pressing the space bar. "Clearing" a problem like this will send it back to the student to rework.

5. From here, you can click on NEXT on the toolbar, or press F2 to go to the next problem needing grading. You can also right-click. Clicking on DONE or pressing the Esc key ends the grading session.

Projects

Students click a button to send completed projects to the teacher. The project icon will not appear in the teacher's Grading Menu until the teacher has graded past the lesson preceding the project assignment. The project icon will appear below the subject icons.

Click on the project icon to open the project. Any grading guidelines will be located near the bottom of the page. Click on the "Report" icon to see the student's work. When you are grading, you can type your comments in a different color (change the font size and color—Format | Font).

Answer Key

To see the answer key in Teacher Mode or Student Review:

1. Hold down KEY on the toolbar, **or**

2. Hold down the Shift key, **or**

3. Press the F5 button (to "lock" the key on the screen)

The answer key will temporarily replace the student answers. If a problem allows text box answers in any order, each tinted box will contain an ellipsis (...), and the alternate answers will be displayed at the bottom of the question, correct answer groups separated by commas. Square brackets [ ] around letters indicate optional text. Curly braces { } indicate a key word in the answer. Generally, only the primary answer is displayed in a textbox; however, alternates are often allowed. Paragraph and reports are teacher graded and often have grading guidelines located below the answer box (paragraphs) or the question (reports).

ENTERING/CHANGING GRADES

Located above each problem is a score box in which the teacher can enter or adjust the grade. The following is a list of grading options:

- **Type a letter grade**: A, B, C, D, P (for Pass, which is the same as A), F or X (X is the same as F); the percentage will automatically be calculated as the highest percent in the grade range. (See grading scale in *School Setup*.)

- **Type in a number** from 0 to 100 percent and the letter grade will automatically be calculated based on the grade scale used in School Setup.

- **Type a fraction**: the percentage will automatically be calculated and a letter grade assigned. Examples: 7/8 or 17/19.

- **Type "s"** skips the problem. Grade will not be included in the total and the problem will be skipped when the student goes through the lesson. Skip can be set at any time, even before the student attempts the problem.

- **Type a space** (press the space bar): indicates the problem is incomplete and clears out the problem score. The problem is automatically sent back to the student to re-work. If you do this, the student will also get another try at any other missed questions.

- **Type "g"** sets the problem to "Gave Up." Students can give up on a problem (using Problem Helps) to stop the problem from being repeated in Focus Learning mode. "Gave Up" is scored the same as a zero (0).

- **Clear (erase) a report** by holding the Shift key and clicking on the Report icon.

IN-DEPTH GRADING

To see all of the problems a student has worked on in a unit:

1. Go to the Teacher Menu.

2. Click on student's name.

3. To open the Unit Grades Menu, select a unit by clicking on the appropriate box in the unit grid near the bottom of the screen (matching subject with unit number). Like a table of contents, the Unit Grades Menu divides the unit into lessons, quizzes, reports, test, and reference. Select any lesson and you will see all the presentations and problems contained in that lesson.

Questions will be highlighted in one of three colors: gray, red, or black. If the problem is highlight in gray, it was "skipped" by either the student or the teacher. Black means the student has answered the problem 100% correctly or has done no work at all in that lesson. Red means the student got less than 100% on the question, gave up, or has started work in the lesson but is not completely finished yet.

Note: The teacher may adjust the scores given by the computer grading system using the grading options listed previously in this chapter.

Clear Entire Lesson/ or Single Problems

The teacher can delete all student work in a lesson and send the lesson back to the student to re-work. Click on Clear to bring up the prompt "Delete Student Work and Grades?" Select YES.

Teachers can also clear a single problem to send back to the student. Simply type a space in the problem score box to clear the grade. **Note:** The student will also be able to work on other incorrect problems when you do this.

Assigned/Skipped/Blocked

Assigned = work sent to student to complete

Skipped = student never sees work

Blocked = work assigned, but the student cannot go into it until the teacher changes the setting to "Assigned."

Note: Switched-On Schoolhouse offers extra projects that are not initially assigned. The teacher can give additional work by assigning these projects. (Click on the button labeled "Skipped" to change it to "Assigned.")

In the Unit Grades Menu, percentage and/or letter grades are posted next to all completed lessons, projects, quizzes and tests. An averaged grade for a unit is posted in the Grading Menu. Students can view their grades through the Schoolwork Menu and Review Menu.

PROBLEM NOTEBOOKS

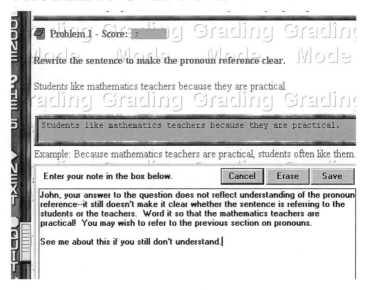

Students and teachers may leave messages for each other attached to specific problems by opening the small notebook next to the problem number. Click on the notebook to open it; type the message; click Save to close. The notebook cover will flap up and down and flash Message if a note has been left. Teachers can use the same notebook to respond to student messages.

Students may also use these problem notebooks to skip a problem they are having trouble with. They can type a message, click on the option "Leave message for Teacher; Skip problem" and the problem will be sent to you to look at. This feature can be disabled in Student Setup.

Note: To send a message to a student, using the problem notebook, clear the scorebox of all characters by clicking in the box and pressing the space bar. The problem will be sent back to the student to rework.

Chapter 5

STUDENT MODE

*Students study and do their
work right on the computer.*

STUDENT MENU

Students use this menu to click open their own
individual Schoolwork Menus. The teacher can assign a
password to each student (see *Student Setup*) to restrict
access to other students' work.

Though the Student Menu is also the doorway to the
Teacher Menu, the teacher's personal password (see
School Setup) denies students access to the Teacher
Mode.

SCHOOLWORK MENU

Start Lessons

All the subjects assigned to the student appear at the
top of the Schoolwork Menu. Students use these
subject icons to access their daily schoolwork. The
subject buttons at the bottom of the menu display the

grades and shortcut to the Review Menu, where the student can study completed lessons.

Starting from the opening Student Menu:

1. Click on student's name.
2. Click on subject bar or project bar to begin work.

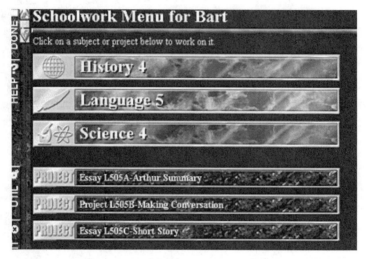

3. Choose from the options given:
   - Send messages to or read messages from the teacher.
   - Click Cancel to return to the Schoolwork Menu.
   - Click Review Previous Lessons to go to the Review Menu.
   - Click Start Lesson to begin work.

Note: Switched-On Schoolhouse places a "bookmark" in the lesson when you exit so you can start up again right where you left off.

Projects

Project bars will periodically be added to the student's Schoolwork Menu and will appear below the subject bars. Projects are labeled by subject name, number, and title. For example, *Essay L505B–Making Conversation* is an essay called "Making Conversation" assigned from 5th grade Language Arts, unit 5, the second essay (B). These projects are also listed with the lessons in the Review Menu. Students may enter and exit projects any number of times until they click on the box at the top of the project page to send the project to the teacher for grading.

View Lesson Plan

Click on View Lesson Plan to see the student's lesson plan. The lesson plan opens in a word processor file that can be printed out. **Note:** The file you see is only a temporary copy. Any changes you make will not be saved.

Unit Grades

The averaged grades for each unit are listed in the grade grid near the bottom of the Schoolwork Menu.

Review Lessons

Students can review their completed lessons by clicking on a unit in the grade grid to open the Review Menu.

Set Theme

Switched-On Schoolhouse has several desktop themes that give a variety of different looks to the program but **do not** affect its operation. To change the desktop theme:

1. Click on student name.
2. Click on Set Theme.
3. Choose a theme and select OK.

Note: Choosing a different theme **WILL NOT** change the program settings, student work, or student grades.

REVIEW MENU

Before they take a quiz or test, students can review work they have completed.

1. Click on the subject/unit button (located in Overview below the subject bars) to go to the Review Menu **OR**

2. Choose Review Previous Lessons from the SOS message system that opens at the start of each lesson, quiz, and test.

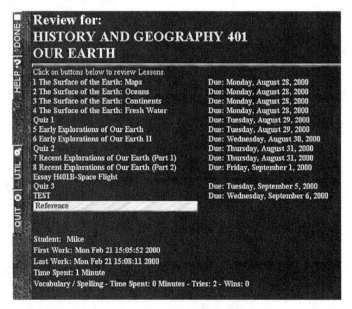

3. Click on the title of a completed lesson

From this menu—which looks like a table of contents—students can look at the lesson presentations and problems. Lessons that have been completed will be listed on buttons. Click on the button to review the lesson. The lessons that have not been completed will be shown without buttons and cannot be viewed.

Answers in completed lessons cannot be changed, but all the questions appear at once rather than one at a time. Incorrectly answered questions are highlighted in red and skipped questions are gray. The final grade for each lesson, quiz, or test is displayed in this menu. Due dates are also shown if the lesson plan has been generated.

Status

In the Review Menu the following information is shown underneath the list of lesson titles:

- when the student first began work in the unit
- when the student last worked in the unit
- total time spent in the unit
- time spent in vocabulary games (number of tries, number of wins)

Autohighlight

Students can use the "autohighlight" feature to quickly find key words in review lessons and thereby increase the organization and efficiency of study time. **Note:** Autohighlight works only in Review and Grading Modes.

To use Autohighlight:

1. Click on a student's name.
2. Choose one of the subject/unit buttons under the Review title.
3. Click on a completed lesson in the Review Menu.
4. Click on UTIL or press the F3 key. In the line labeled "Autohighlight" type in a keyword or phrase. Click

on **Find.** All occurrences of that word or phrase will be highlighted.

Chapter 6

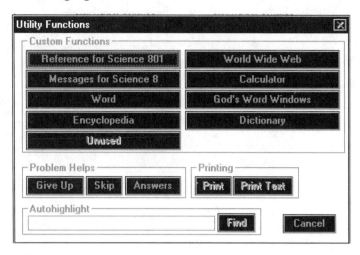

ACTIVITIES

*Students are immersed in the
subject and take an active
part in their learning through
interactivity.*

Lessons are supplemented by diagrams, pictures, and
multimedia interactions. Students read the information
then click on NEXT (F2) to see more information or
begin a set of problems. After answering individual
problems, students click on NEXT and their answers are
instantly graded. When Focus Learning is used, students
will remain in a lesson until all the problems are
answered correctly. See *Problems* for more information.

MULTIMEDIA

Education comes alive through multimedia! Science
experiments performed by our in-house science team
are caught on video. In geometry, three-dimensional
objects are illustrated rotating in space. Video clips
illustrating events in the Bible, literature, and history
have been obtained from our extensive video library
and are used to enhance the curriculum. Sound

captures of the vocabulary words allow students to hear how each word is pronounced, and spelling tests are given directly by the computer. Students can print charts or forms for various activities such as drawing graphs or conducting surveys.

Sound Clips

Sound clips are indicated by words in blue type or by a gold speaker symbol located at the bottom right corner of a graphic (see above).

- Click on the word in blue type to hear the sound (vocabulary pronunciation, poetry, Scripture readings, etc.) **Note:** Sorting and matching problems also use blue type, but no sound will be heard when you click on these words. Instead, the word will be highlighted in black.

- If you see a gold speaker symbol at the bottom right hand corner of a graphic, click on the graphic—you may have to wait a few seconds— and the sound will play.

Vocabulocity and Alpha 14

Switched-On Schoolhouse brings vocabulary drill into the world of science fiction with Vocabulocity and its sequel, Alpha 14. Students read a vocabulary definition, fly through a 3-D world (with many distractions), and attempt to choose the correct vocabulary word to match the definition by moving the mouse pointer to open ports or air locks. These are more than mere matching games—students have to remember their definitions. These activities are ungraded; game statistics are recorded in the Unit Grades and Review Mode screens.

VOCABULARY

alphabet	A set of letters used in writing and reading.
consonant	Any letter that is not a vowel.
correct	Free from mistakes; right, not wrong.
grammar	A study of the uses of words.
punctuation mark	A mark used for sentences.
symbol	A mark that stands for something else.
vowels	Letters that are not consonants, a, e, i, o, u, and sometimes y.

Vocabulary / Spelling Activities
Click Here For Vocabulocity
Click Here For Spelling Bee!
Click Here For Alpha14!

Note: Vocabulocity must be installed on your computer in order to play it. (See *Installation Options.*)

Spelling Bee

Students can practice their spelling in a race against time. Each round is taken from the current vocabulary or spelling list. Students can play multiple games in order to beat their time. The game continues until all words have been spelled correctly. This activity is ungraded.

Note: Spelling Bee must be installed on your computer in order to play it. (See *Installation Options.*)

The program compiles statistics on the amount of time spent in vocabulary/spelling games as well as the number of tries, and number of wins. Go to the Review Menu (for Students) or the Unit Grades Menu (for

Teachers) to see these. Vocabulocity, Alpha 14, and Spelling Bee can be disabled in Student Setup.

Animations and Video Clips

Click on the picture.

Computer animations or video clips are marked by a gold video camera icon located at the bottom right hand corner of a graphic or picture.

- Click anywhere on the picture to play the video clip one time.

- Click with the right mouse button to play the video continuously.

- Hold the shift key down while clicking (with either right or left mouse button) to play the video full screen.

- To stop the video, click anywhere with the mouse button.

Slide Shows

Slide Shows are a combination of graphics and sound. Students control the pace of the presentation by clicking on the graphic when they are ready for the next picture. Full-screen slide shows let the student scroll over large graphics (the student moves the mouse pointer to any edge of the screen).

Animazing

Animazing presentations are a cross between a slide show and a video clip. Click to start these presentations and they run on their own like a video; however, the video symbol does not appear.

Tiny Tutors

Tiny Tutor Screens

Like a sidebar in a magazine, Tiny Tutors highlight interesting information, tie concepts together, and direct the student's attention to important or difficult concepts in the curriculum. Click on the graphic to start and stop the video.

Print-out Feature

Print-outs (optional) are available for students to help them complete some of their projects. Instructions direct the student to click on a graphic or words in blue type to print items such as graph paper, star charts, or detailed instructions.

Internet Links

If you have Internet access, your students can visit the World-Wide Web through the UTIL button on the toolbar or from within the curriculum wherever they see an animated "WWW" icon. Clicking on WWW links in the curriculum will start the browser at a designated web page. You can set up the link to your web browser in School Setup.

Review Prompt

Before a quiz or test begins, the message box prompt will open with the question: "Have you reviewed for this quiz?" Options are given to Cancel, Review for Quiz, or Start Quiz. Selecting Review for Quiz sends the student to the Review Menu. Selecting Cancel sends the student back to the Schoolwork Menu. Selecting Start Quiz begins the quiz.

PROBLEMS

Timed Problems

Some problems are equipped with timers. When the time runs out the answers get graded! Students will be warned in advance of timed problems, and they will be able to see a "counter."

Problem Helps

When Focus Learning is on, students must correctly answer all the problems in the lesson. If there is a problem that the student just cannot get, he has the option to use Problem Helps. Teachers must supply the password first in order for students to use the following three options: **Give Up** (get a score of zero), **Skip** (question not included in the grading), or **Answers** (displays the correct answer).

Click on UTIL in the toolbar (or press F3) to bring up the Utilities options. The Teacher Password must be set in School Setup (Teacher Mode) before Problem Helps can be used.

Problem Notebooks

Another way for students to work past a problem is through 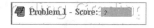 the Problem Notebook. Click on the notebook next to the score box. Type a message; then select "Leave message for teacher; skip problem." The advantage of using the notebook is that the student can continue working without waiting for the teacher to come type the password (as with *Problem Helps*, see above). Teachers will be alerted to any messages by a "Needs Grading" notice on the subject icon. This feature can be disabled in Student Setup by selecting the box labeled: "Disable leave message for teacher; skip problem."

If the "Leave message for teacher; skip problem" feature is turned off, students and teachers may still leave messages attached to the specific problems. Click on the notebook to open; type the message; click Save to close. The notebook cover will flap up and down and flash the word MESSAGE when a note has been left. Click Erase to delete the message.

Note: The program will not alert the teacher to any messages if the "Leave message for teacher; skip problem" function is turned off.

Crossword Puzzles

Crossword puzzles are set up in a simple grid pattern using letters and numbers. Clues help the students find the answers. Press the up/down arrow keys to type a word vertically; press the right/left arrow keys to type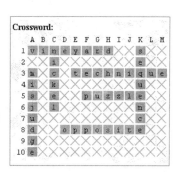

a word horizontally. Two- or three-word answers are separated by blank white spaces.

Drag-and-Drop

Used to label maps and diagrams or to set up algebraic equations, drag-and-drop graphics allow students to "pick up" items from a menu, drag them to the main graphic, and drop them into position. The menu of icons to drag is located below the main graphic.

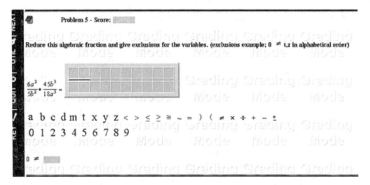

Click on the selected item and, holding down the mouse button, slide the mouse to move the item to the correct position. To drop an item, release the mouse button. Dragging a selected item off the main graphic or out of the active space will delete it. Dropping a new item onto an already placed item will replace the old. Menu items can be used more than once.

Dynamic Learning Activities (DLAs)

Dynamic Learning Activities:

- give students practice at a skill
- teach the proper way to complete a problem
- help teachers diagnose student errors

Each DLA has a help screen to explain how to work the activity.

The States Game

Choose the correct state of the union after reviewing clues such as bordering states and major cities, including that state's capital. A correct answer gives the student the chance to place the state in its correct location on a United States map.

The Chemistry Game

Balance equations by selecting the correct combination of numbered beakers and then "mixing" their contents. This game appears in both graded and ungraded versions.

The Chalkboard

Step up to the virtual chalkboard to work math problems. The game provides instant feedback, showing student errors and modeling correct processing skills. Versions of this game—both with and without decimals—include addition, subtraction, multiplication, and division.

Timeline

Explore a wider historical context while memorizing important dates. Click on a date (where linked) in a lesson to read about key historical events surrounding the lesson discussion or get the bird's-eye view—from Creation to the Twenty-first Century.

Teachers have three options when reviewing student work in DLAs:

1. Click on the DLA graphic to see student's work.
2. Shift-click on the DLA graphic to see the correct answer.

3. Right-click on the DLA graphic to run the activity (as though you are the student).

Note: DLAs in quizzes and tests are not compatible with Open Page or Open Book modes because the program grades these activities immediately. When the program is set to run in these modes, the DLAs will not appear.

Matching

Students can move the words in blue type in the first column to match the definitions or descriptions in the second column. Students click on the word they want to

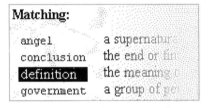

move (it will be highlighted in black). Then, they click on the location where they want to place the word. The highlighted word will then change places with the word in that location. Students can de-select a word (without moving it) by clicking on it again. Students continue moving the words around until they have matched all the words with the descriptions.

Multiple Choice

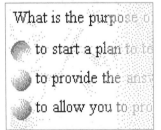

Students can select only one answer in multiple choice problems. When one round button is selected, all the others are deselected. Students may select and deselect a choice any number of times before clicking NEXT. Be careful — sometimes the best answer is "all of the above" or "none of the above."

Multiple Choice Text

A blank textbox that automatically produces 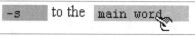 a word when you click on it indicates a multiple choice text question. Possible answers are already typed in the textbox. Students click in the box to cycle through possible answers. The problem is completed when the correct answer is displayed.

Multiple Choice Graphics

Students click on the graphic to reveal another, slightly different graphic. The various graphics will continuously loop as students click on them. The student stops clicking when the correct graphic is displayed.

Paragraphs

> One of the greatest developments in the field of education was achieved in the late 20th century...Switched-On Schoolhouse.

Paragraph boxes are used to answer problems that require short sentence and essay answers. These paragraphs are sent to the teacher for grading so they will not appear again with Focus Learning.

WARNING! Once students click on NEXT, they will not be able to get back to the paragraph box to change the answer.

Selections

Similar to multiple choice problems, selections allow students to choose none, one, or more answers. Click on as many boxes as apply to the problem. The students may

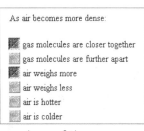

select and deselect a choice any number of times before clicking on NEXT.

Sorting

To alphabetize or place events in the proper order, students click to move the word in blue type. When a word is selected, it will be highlighted in black. Students click on the location where they want the word to go, and the highlighted word will change places with that word. Students continue moving the words around until they have the correct order. Sorting is similar to matching, but in quizzes and tests, sorted answers are graded according to their sequence rather than their specific position in a list. This means students receive partial credit for partially correct answers.

Text

Tom has discovered the most　efficie_　way to complete the project.

Switched-On Schoolhouse employs an intelligent scripting system which allows for a variety of correct answers. Students apply analytical problem solving skills rather than rote memorization. Switched-On Schoolhouse even checks for spelling and can be set to subtract percentage points for misspelled words. With many other features working behind the scenes, the automatic grading system promotes the dynamic interaction that a full curriculum demands.

A narrow, tinted box indicates a text entry blank. Most blanks require only one word or number, but some may require a very short phrase.

To move from one box to the next, click on the desired box or use the Enter or Tab keys. To delete letters use the Delete or Backspace keys. To insert letters, click on the box where you want to put the letters and begin typing. The other letters will move to the right to make room for any inserts. If you type too many letters, the end letters will be deleted.

Preloaded. Sometimes the text entry boxes already have words or sentences typed in them. These problems generally require the student to correct something in that word or sentence. In these problems, grading is very exact, right down to punctuation, spelling, and capitalization.

Spelling. The teacher can set the program to allow for some misspelled answers; the question will be graded as correct, but marks will be taken off for incorrect spelling (School Setup and Student Setup).

True/False

Click on the T/F box to change back and forth between TRUE and FALSE.

Projects

As students go through their daily work, projects are periodically assigned. These projects contain a set of instructions or questions and are graded solely by the teacher.

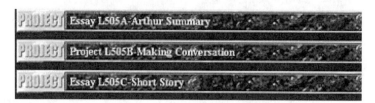

PROJECT Essay L505A-Arthur Summary

PROJECT Project L505B-Making Conversation

PROJECT Essay L505C-Short Story

Students access their projects by clicking on the project bars that appear on their desktops. To send reports to the teacher for grading, students click on the box labeled "Check here when your project is complete." Until this box is checked, students may enter and leave projects at any time.

Extra and Special Projects

Extra projects are initially skipped (unassigned). The teacher can give  additional work assignments by assigning these projects. Teachers may create their own projects to assign to students, as well. In Teacher Mode, go to the Unit Grades Menu for a student and assign the "Special Project" listed near the bottom of the table of contents.

1. Go to Teacher Mode.

2. Click on student's name.

3. Click on a subject/unit button located under the Overview title.

4. Click on the Special Project button, then click on the small notepad at the top.

5. Type the new project instructions here. Click Save to keep the instructions. Click Erase if you want to delete the instructions. Assign the project in the Unit Grades Menu.

Reports

Reports are found within projects. Clicking on the NEW REPORT icon launches a word processor where students may answer the given question(s). Students may enter and leave the report at any time by saving any work, closing out of the word processor and clicking DONE or pressing the ESC key. Once a report has been started, NEW REPORT will be labeled OPEN REPORT. To send the report to the teacher for grading, students click on the box labeled "Check here when your project is complete."

Student Note: When you have finished a report and exit your word processor, be sure to save your work. Simply click on Save. DO NOT click on "Save As" and change the file name. Switched-On Schoolhouse links to the **original** file name.

Teacher Note: The project icon will not appear in the teacher's Grading Menu until the teacher has graded **past** the lesson preceding the project assignment.

Chapter 7

TECHNICAL INFORMATION

This section will answer many of your questions about the Switched-On Schoolhouse Program.

SYSTEM RECOMMENDATIONS

CD-ROM Multimedia PC:
Pentium 133 or better
16 Megabytes of RAM or better
16-Bit sound card capable of 22,050 KHz or better
SVGA Video Card capable of 640x480 by 256 colors
4X CD-ROM drive or better
Windows 95 or 98 (NOT Windows NT)

INSTALLATION REQUIREMENTS

Minimal installation requires 10 MB of hard drive space (does not include games, intro videos, or desktop themes).

Small installation requires 35 MB of hard drive space (does not include intro videos or desktop themes).

Full installation requires 93 MB of hard drive space.

DISPLAY

You should set your display to at least 256 colors (16-bit color works).

FREQUENTLY ASKED QUESTIONS

This section is divided into subtopics to help you find answers quickly. The categories are: Technical, Multimedia, and General.

Technical

• *Why does the data take up so much hard drive space?*

Your computer's operating system contains a "clustering" mechanism that automatically designates a certain amount of space for each file, even though that file has very little data in it. Each subject uses about 200 files. If you right-click on one of these files and look at "Properties" (in Windows 95/98), you will be able to see the actual amount of data the file contains and the amount of space it is taking up on the hard drive because of the clustering. The amount of space will be from four to sixteen megabytes per student per year (five subjects). However, you should be able to copy that same data onto a single floppy.

• *How do I add another subject?*

1. Go to Teacher Mode.
2. Click on School Setup.
3. Click on Add Subject and follow the on-screen instructions.

Note: Remember to assign the subject to your student in Student Setup.

• *How do I maintain back-ups of the students' work?*

Use the Back Up/ Restore function to do this. (See *Back-ups* in Chapter 1.)

• *My student is going to be moving to another computer. How do I transfer the grade files from my computer to the new one?*

Use the Back Up Data function (See Back-ups in Chapter 1) to obtain a back-up of your student data. Install Switched-On Schoolhouse onto the new computer. Use the Restore Data function to restore the student's work on the new computer.

• *I assigned a subject that I don't have the CD-ROM for and now I'm stuck. How do I get out?*

Hold down the CTRL key and click on the student name in Teacher Mode. This takes you directly to the Student Setup where you can un-assign any missing subjects.

• *My CD-ROM drive letter has changed and Switched-On Schoolhouse isn't working anymore. How do I fix it?*

First, make a back-up of all the student grade files. Then run the remove.bat program off any current SOS CD-ROM. Answer "Y" to all questions. Reinstall Switched-On Schoolhouse and use the Restore Data function to restore your students' data.

Multimedia

• *How do I stop a video or sound link from playing?*

Click anywhere with the mouse button.

• *Aren't there supposed to be videos that show the grade at the end of the lesson?*

These videos must be installed on your computer and "Letter Grades" must be selected in School Setup.

- *Why do the video clips run "choppy" or slowly sometimes?*

There may be many reasons for this:

- insufficient processor speed (slow computer)
- video card quality
- running multiple programs and using RAM elsewhere
- CD drive is slow (less than 4X)
- CD drive is having trouble reading the CD
- in a networked situation, a slow network server

- *Why does nothing happen when I click on a blue word (sound link) or graphic with a video camera or speaker symbol?*

Sometimes the videos and sound links take a few moments to load. If you click on the mouse button again while you are waiting for the multimedia to start, you stop the video from playing. Click *once*, then wait for the multimedia to play. Also see "Why does the computer hang or crash on some videos?" below. If the multimedia still will not play, contact Technical Support at 1-866-444-4498.

- *Why does the computer hang or crash on some videos?*

Reason 1: You might have bad RAM or not enough RAM. This will slow the computer down. If you have less than 16 MB of RAM, try adding more.

Reason 2: This may be a problem for some Windows 95 users due to a problem with video compression. Try reinstalling the multimedia from your Windows 95/98 installation disks. To do this you will need to uninstall all your multimedia using "add-remove" programs in your control panel:

1. Open Control Panel. Double-click on Add/Remove Programs, choose the Windows Setup tab.

2. Scroll down to Multimedia and uncheck it. When you close these windows, your multimedia will be disabled.

3. You must now insert your Windows CD. Go back through these steps and recheck Multimedia to reinstall it.

4. Restart the computer.

General

• *What is the difference between the "A" disk and the "B" (or "C") disks?*

The "A" disk contains the installation program and the first few units of the subject. "B" and "C" disks

contain the later units of the subject. Switched-On Schoolhouse will prompt you as to which disk you need to have in the CD drive. Always use the "A" disk to install the program or to install the subject.

• *How do I print the curriculum?*

You can print only while you are in Teacher Mode. Simply hold down the CTRL key and press the P key or click on UTIL on the toolbar. Select Print or Print Text.

• *Do I have to listen to the introduction every time I begin the program?*

No. Click the mouse button at any time during the opening animation to stop the introduction.

• *Why aren't there any subject bars (icons) displayed in the Schoolwork Menu?*

Check the settings in Student Setup (found on the Grading Menu). Subjects must be assigned for the icon to appear on the student's Schoolwork Menu.

- *Why is an answer marked correct when it is different from the answer key?*

The answer key shows the most common or expected answer. Other possible answers have been scripted into the answer key but are not displayed.

- *Why is an answer marked wrong when it is the same as the answer key?*

The answer is not the same as the answer key. This confusion may occur with certain types of questions. Some questions already have text in the answer boxes and students are required to add punctuation, change spelling, or some other such activity. The grading system in these cases is very exact. If there are extra punctuation marks or the capitalization is different, the answer will be graded as "Incorrect."

- *Why do the reports come up empty when I click on them to grade?*

Your student changed the name of the report file (i.e. chose "Save As" then changed the file name). Switched-On Schoolhouse links to the **original** file name. Have your student find that file (through your word processor), make a copy of the text and paste it back in the Report, click on Save.

- *How does the student get past a problem that keeps coming back (when Focus Learning is selected)?*

The student can give up on the problem by clicking on UTIL on the toolbar. A dialog box will open, giving the student Problem Helps. To skip or give up on the problem, the teacher must type in the password (set in School Setup).

Another way to skip a problem is through the Problem Notebook. Click on the small notebook near the problem number and choose the "Leave message for teacher; skip problem" option. **Note:** This option can be disabled in Student Setup.

- *Why does nothing happen when I click on the World-Wide Web links in the curriculum?*

1. You must have your own Internet connection from a service provider for the links to work. Switched-On Schoolhouse has links set up to the Web but is not a service provider.

2. There might be something wrong with the location of your web browser. Switched-On Schoolhouse does not include a web browser.

- *How do I delete a student?*

In Teacher Mode, hold down the Shift key and click on the student's name or go to Student Setup and click on Delete This Student.

- *I forgot my Teacher Password. Is there a way to find out what it was?*

Hold down the shift key and click on the "Go To Teacher Mode" icon. This will erase the teacher's password.

- *When do the Past Due notices get updated?*

Past Due notices for a student are automatically updated whenever teachers go into the Grading Menu for that student. **Note:** Lesson plans must be created in order to set up due dates.

- *Why do the project icons not appear in teacher mode?*

The project icon will not appear in the teacher's Grading Menu until the teacher has graded past the lesson preceding the project assignment,

- *How do I uninstall the program?*

Run the install.exe program off any current SOS CD-ROM. Select uninstall.

- *What about Distance Learning and the OnLine Academies?*

Alpha Omega Academy On-Line can be reached at:

- Web site: www.WelcomeToClass.com
- E-mail: online@aopub.com
- Phone: 1-877-688-2652
- Fax: 1-480-893-6112

TROUBLESHOOTING

- *Windows Help Menu*

The Windows 95/98 Help menu is a useful tool to help you correct problems associated with the computer, rather than with the program. Under the Start menu, select Help, then click on the Contents tab. Double-click on Troubleshooting. If your question is not listed, click on the Index tab and type in a keyword. You can also get online help at www.Microsoft.com.

We encourage you to use the program Help File to answer any questions you may have about Switched-On Schoolhouse. If you still have questions or problems, please visit our web site at:

aop.com/HomeSchool/TechSupport/

- *I have problems installing the program.*

Check to see if you have enough hard drive space. See System Recommendations.

- *I installed the subject but my student can't access it.*

You must assign the subject to each student in the Student Setup on the Grading menu.

- *When I scroll down the page, the writing gets all jumbled and mixed around.*

Try exiting other programs that may be running at the same time, or reducing your screen size, or increasing the amount of your computer's hardware RAM.

- *I can't scroll to the right.*

You will need to turn off Autohide on your taskbar.

1. Right-click on the taskbar.

2. Select Properties.

3. Deselect Autohide.

- *The program randomly freezes.*

First try running Scandisk on the hard drive (Start | Programs | Accessories | System Tools). If you still have a problem, try running Disk Defragmenter. Still problems? Turn the Hardware Acceleration down to none (right-click on My Computer | left click on Properties | click on the Performance tab | click on the Graphics button | turn the Hardware acceleration down to none.)

- *I'm getting general protection faults and the program crashes when the screen saver comes on.*

Exit all other programs and turn off the screen saver. You may also need to increase the amount of your computer's hardware RAM.

- *I've set up the lesson plans, but the due dates and Past Due notices are wrong.*

Check the calendar setting on your computer. Make sure that your computer is set to the current date. (For

Windows 95, go the Start Menu | Settings | Control Panel. Double-click on Date/Time. Make necessary changes.

• *I have problems printing the lessons.*

Try printing again, and when the main print screen comes up:

1. Change the DPI setting to the lowest possible.

2. Change your color printer setting to black and white, grayscale, or monochrome.

3. If you have a print quality button, set it on Draft, or the lowest possible.

4. If you have a button for graphics, set it on Coarse.

If the above did not work, load (from your Windows 95 or 98 CD) a lower-level driver than what your printer is. For example, if you have an HP Deskjet 560, select the driver for the HP Deskjet 320. To load a new driver:

1. Insert your Windows CD and click on Start.

2. Go to Settings/Printers/Add Printer and click NEXT.

3. Choose Local Printer and click NEXT.

4. Find your printer, select the lower-level driver, and click NEXT.

5. Choose LPT I (or whatever port your printer is on and click NEXT.

6. You do not want to use the new drivers as the default drivers. Click NEXT.

7. You do not need to print a test page. Click NEXT.

8. When the drivers are installed, go back to SOS and try printing again. At the main print screen, click on Setup, then on Specific Printer.

9. Select the printer you just installed and click Print.

• *My student cannot go past a quiz or test.*

A quiz or test could lock up the program if there has been a combination of Open Book testing with regular testing. For example: the student started to take a quiz or test in Open Book mode but left the test unfinished. The teacher, meanwhile, cancelled the Open Book test (deselected it in Student Setup). The student will not be able to go back into the test or go past the test. To correct, the teacher can either clear the test for the student to redo, or select Open Book again and allow the student to go back in and finish the test.

ERROR MESSAGES

• *Dek error.*

1. Right-click on your SOS icon on your desktop. Go to Properties, then Shortcut.

2. Make sure the line labeled "Target" says: C:\SOS\SOS.EXE (or whatever your drive is).

If this is not the problem, then you will need to uninstall and reinstall the program.

1. Make a back-up of all the student grade files.

2. Run the install.exe program off any current SOS CD-ROM. Select uninstall.

3. Reinstall Switched-On Schoolhouse and use the Restore Data function to restore your students' data.

• *Cannot Load Lesson Counts (when trying to generate a lesson plan).*

1. Double-click on My Computer/double-click on your C:\ drive/Double-click on the SOS folder/double-click on the Work folder.

2. Inside the Work folder, delete the folder called List.

3. Immediately run SOS. Clear the Calendar, reset it, then generate the lesson plan.

4. Insert CDs if required.

• *Work or Grade File Altered*

Solution A:

1. Go to Teacher Mode.

2. Back up student's work.

3. Click on the student's name.

4. Under the Overview section on this screen, choose the subject/unit that the student is working in.

5. Clear the last completed lesson. Do this in all subjects that are giving this message.

If the above did not work, try a more drastic and time-consuming approach.

Solution B:

1. Go to Start/Find/Files or Folders.

2. In the named box, type *.GRD

3. For the Look In box, click on Browse.

4. Browse in the C:\SOS\WORK folder (if this is your drive letter.

5. Click on Find Now.

6. Delete all files that end with .GRD.

This will delete the grades for your students but **not** the work. When your student goes back into the program and starts a lesson, he will go to the very first lesson. (Don't panic—the work is still there.) Press NEXT (F2) through the lessons until the student is up to date.

• *No Body*

See Solution B for Work or Grade File Altered (above).

• *This file is not a valid WIN32 application.*

1. Clean the CD carefully with a soft, clean cloth.

2. Clean your CD drive. (You can buy an inexpensive CD cleaner at most computer stores.)

• *Cannot Open for Reading/Writing*

Install Switched-On Schoolhouse again (you do not have to uninstall first). Choose "minimal" installation. This will re-copy the Switched-On Schoolhouse code to your hard drive, not affecting your students' work.

• *Your Sound Card Is Not Working*

Restart your computer and run the program again. If there is still a problem:

1. Go to Start/Settings/Control Panel/Sounds

2. In the box labeled Schemes, select Windows Default None

3. Click OK.

4. Restart your computer and try again.

• *Not Enough RAM (while trying to restore data)*

Your floppy disk is probably bad. Try restoring one subject at a time.

• *Insert another disk (continually asks this when trying to Restore Data)*

One of the files is probably too large to fit onto a floppy disk. Try running the backup to a hard drive or looking for a huge file in your student data (C:\SOS\WORK).

• *Error in Compression Codes*

There is a problem with your Windows file. Contact

Microsoft to have the problem fixed.

- *General Protection Fault/Illegal Operation (when trying to grade)*

Delete the grade file in the lesson you are having trouble with. To do this:

1. You need to know the student number and where the problem is (subject, unit number, and lesson number). You will find this information in the Unit Grades Menu.

2. Exit Switched-On Schoolhouse.

3. Double-click on My Computer | C:\drive | SOS Folder | Work Folder | the folder with that student's student number/the subject that has the problem/the unit number where the problem is.

4. Right-click on the .GRD file of the lesson where the problem is (i.e., Lesson 2 would be L2.GRD). Click on Delete.

5. Go back into Switched-On Schoolhouse. The problem should be corrected.

ONLINE ACADEMIES

There are a number of on-line academies using the Switched-On Schoolhouse. Students link up to the schools over the Internet. The academies keep track of the students' progress, grade their work, and offer personalized assistance.

Since SOS comes complete with an internal messaging system, the student can request help about the subject in general or about specific questions within the curriculum. Teachers with expertise in the subject will respond to the students' questions and help them work through problem areas.

How Does it work?

Students do their schoolwork at home on the computer. At the end of the day, they link up to the Academy and send their work to their teachers. At the same time, any grading or tutoring the teachers have done gets sent back to the student.

The OnLine Academies offer:

- Placement testing
- Progress reports and report cards
- Official transcripts
- Permanent records
- Graduation credits

Alpha Omega Academy On-Line can be reached at:

- Web site: www.WelcomeToClass.com
- E-mail: online@aopub.com
- Phone: 1-877-688-2652
- Fax: 1-480-893-6112

Chapter 8

LIFEPAC COMPARISON

Compare the Switched-On Schoolhouse scope and sequence to the LIFEPAC scope and sequence.

Switched-On Schoolhouse originally drew from the LIFEPAC curriculum. Authors and editors have since updated the content, re-written sections, and improved the material with multimedia presentations.

The following tables display Switched-On Schoolhouse units under the headings of corresponding LIFEPAC numbers when they differ from old diagnostic test LIFEPAC numbers. The numbers inside the grid tell you which SOS units contain the information found in the current LIFEPAC unit in that column.

Note: You can find the detailed Scope and Sequence for Switched-On Schoolhouse on each CD-ROM. In the Teacher Menu, click on Scope and Sequence to open the file in your word processor. The Scope and Sequence document is a large file, but you can copy and paste the information you need onto another page.

Note: Older versions of LIFEPACs may not match these tables.

LP #	301	302	303	304	305	306	307	308	309	310
Bible	304			301						
History	304	301 302	302	306	302 305	303	305	307		
Lang.										
Math										
Science										

LP #	401	402	403	404	405	406	407	408	409	410
Bible										
History										
Lang.										
Math										
Science										

LP #	501	502	503	504	505	506	507	508	509	510
Bible										
History		503	504, 505, 506	505	504					
Lang.										
Math										
Science										

LP #	601	602	603	604	605	606	607	608	609	610
Bible										
History										
Lang.	607 609	602 603	604	601,602 603,605 606	602,603 604,606	608	601,603 604	601,602 605	604 609	
Math	601 602	602 608	603 608 609		604 605 608	601,603 604,606 608	605 606	607 608	601 604 605	
Science										

LP #	701	702	703	704	705	706	707	708	709	710
Bible										
History										
Lang.										
Math	703	704	707	702 705	701	705	706	709	708	
Science										

*Newer printings of LIFEPAC History & Geography now follow the same Scope and Sequence as Switched-On Schoolhouse.

LP #	801	802	803	804	805	806	807	808	809	810
Bible										
History			803, 804					808, 809		
Lang.										
Math	801,809 805	801,809 802	809 802	803	804	801,809 810		806	808	806 810
Science										

LP #	901	902	903	904	905	906	907	908	909	910
Bible										
History	904	905	906	910	907	901	903	908	902	909
Lang.				905	904					
Math										
Science					907	908	906	905		

LP #	1001	1002	1003	1004	1005	1006	1007	1008	1009	1010
Bible										
History										
Lang.	1005	1001 1004	1002	1005 1009	1003	1001 1003	1003 1008	1006	1007	
Math	801 1001		1003 1007	1004 1007		1006 1007	1007 1008	1009	NEW	
Science										

LP #	1101	1102	1103	1104	1105	1106	1107	1108	1109	1110
Bible										
History										
Lang.										
Math										
Science										

LP #	1201	1202	1203	1204	1205	1206	1207	1208	1209	1210
Bible										
History										1209, 1210	1211
Lang.									1209	1208	
Math										
Science										

Chapter 9

OUR PHILOSOPHY OF EDUCATION

The following are the principles that we use in designing our learning products.

FIVE KEY ELEMENTS TO OUR PHILOSOPHY OF EDUCATION

Biblical Basis

We believe that the Word of God is the standard and foundation for the truth. Our educational resources will not contradict that which is written in the Bible.

Reasoning Skills

Curriculum questions are designed to develop a student's reasoning abilities. We go beyond typical recall questions like true and false, multiple choice, and fill in the blank. Questions develop analytical skills through the requirement of brief answers, essays, and experiments. Thus, the curriculum targets memory and higher order skills.

Integrated Subject Material

We believe ALL subject material should be integrated to help the student understand that life is not "compartmentalized."

Mathematical skills are necessary in science.

Scientific research is rich in historical data.

Language Arts is valuable in communicating God's Word, God's history, and God's science.

Personalized Instruction

We believe that a student excels in learning when an instructor is involved. Our curriculum is not a self-study course and the questions require personal instruction. We also believe it is the parents' responsibility as well as a personal blessing to instruct their children.

Mastery Learning

Mastery learning is based on the principle that a student must master the content and skills of a lesson before progressing to the next. When the student begins the curriculum, it is essential that he begin at his present "learning skill level." Diagnostic testing plays an important role in assessing a child's scholastic ability.

Chapter 10

SOFTWARE LICENSE AGREEMENT

By installing this software package, or using or allowing others to use the contents of this package, you are agreeing to the terms, conditions, disclaimer of warranty, and limitations of remedies set forth below.

SOFTWARE LICENSE AGREEMENT, DISCLAIMER OF WARRANTY, AND LIMITATION OF REMEDIES

By installing this software package, or using or allowing others to use the contents of this package, you are agreeing to the terms, conditions, disclaimer of warranty and limitations of remedies set forth below.

Software License Agreement

1. Alpha Omega Publications. "Alpha Omega" does not sell any title or ownership rights or interests in or to the enclosed software program. By purchasing this product, you are only purchasing a non-exclusive license to use the enclosed software program. Alpha Omega (or other parties from whom it has acquired the software program) reserves and retains all other rights, title and interests (including copyrights, patents, trademarks and service marks) in and to the enclosed software program. The purchase price paid for this product constitutes a license fee, in part, for the use of the enclosed software program. The other part of the purchase price covers the enclosed physical optical disk or other physical media on which the software program is recorded or fixed. Although the purchaser of this product will not own the enclosed software program, the purchaser will own the physical optical disk or other physical media on which the software program is recorded or fixed.

2. The allowed use of the enclosed software program under this License Agreement is limited to the following:

   a. The software program may only be used in a single computer (i.e., with a single CPU) at a single location. The enclosed software program, as recorded and fixed on the enclosed optical disk (CD-ROM) or other media, may be physically transferred from one computer to another as long as the software program is only used in one computer at a time. The enclosed software program may not be electronically transferred from one computer to another (over a network or otherwise).

   b. The copying, reproduction, duplication, translation, reverse engineering, adaptation, decompilation, disassembly, reverse assembly, modification or alteration of the enclosed software program (or accompanying written materials) is expressly prohibited without the prior written consent of Alpha Omega, regardless of the form or media in/on which the originals or copies may exist. The merger or inclusion of the enclosed software program (or accompanying written materials) with any other computer program, and the creation of derivative works or programs from the enclosed software program (or accompanying written materials), is also expressly prohibited without the prior written consent of Alpha Omega.

   c. The enclosed software program is licensed to the purchaser of this product, and may not be rented, leased, sold, assigned, transferred, re-licensed, sub-licensed or conveyed for any monetary or other consideration. Any attempted rental, lease, sale, assignment, transfer, re-license, sub-license, conveyance, gift or other disposition of the enclosed software in violation of this license is null and void. Any violation of this License Agreement by the purchaser or any user or recipient of the enclosed software program may also violate applicable copyright law and could result in civil and/or criminal prosecution. You may be held legally responsible for any copyright infringement that is caused, encouraged or allowed by your failure to abide by the terms of this License Agreement.

3. This License Agreement shall remain in effect until terminated. This License Agreement will terminate automatically without notice from Alpha Omega in the event any provision of this License Agreement is violated by the purchaser or any other recipient or user of the enclosed software program. Upon termination, the purchaser, or any other party in possession of this product, shall destroy the enclosed software program and all accompanying written materials.

4. Alpha Omega may create, from time to time, updated versions of the enclosed software program. At its option, Alpha Omega will make such updates available at a cost, and on such terms and conditions, as Alpha Omega considers appropriate in its sole discretion.

Disclaimer Of Warranty And Limitation Of Remedies

The enclosed software program and accompanying written materials (including instructions for use) are provided "as is" and "with all faults", and without express or implied warranty of any kind. Further, Alpha Omega does not warrant, guarantee or make any representations regarding the use or the results of use of the enclosed software or written materials in terms of correctness accuracy, reliability, currentness,

January 1, 2001.

INDEX

H

I

Internet Links, 70, 82, 105, 123

K

Key, 15
Keyboard Controls, 15, 39, 48–51

L

Language Arts, 8, 39, 41, 44, 81, 140
Leave Message, 50, 82, 107, 123
Legal Information, 141
Lesson Blocking, 38, 68, 85, 92
Lessons, 42, 47, 64, 95, 97
Lesson Plans, 14, 36, 78–79, 83, 97, 125, 127
Letter Grades, 63–64, 90, 93
License Agreement, 141

M

Map Network Drive, 32
Matching, 110, 112
Mathematics, 39, 44, 140
Menus, 17–24
    Grading, 19–21, 72–75, 84
    Review, 23, 51–52, 54, 98–99, 106
    School Setup, 11–12, 61–72
    Schoolwork, 22–23, 47, 51–52, 93–95, 122
    Student, 21–22, 47, 95–96
    Student Setup, 74–75
    Teacher, 18, 57
    Unit Grades, 20, 84
Messages
    boxes, 48
    problem notebook, 93
Multimedia
    animation, 104–105
    Animazing, 105
    Internet (WWW), 70, 82, 105, 123
    print-outs, 105
    review prompt, 106
    slide shows, 104
    sound clips, 102
    Spelling Bee, 103
    Tiny Tutors, 105

Q

R

W